Eat Like a Maisel

Eat Like a Maisel

The Unofficial Cookbook for Fans of *The Marvelous Mrs. Maisel*

Anthony LeDonne

Skyhorse Publishing

Skyhorse Publishing books may be purchased in bulk at special discounts for sales promotion, corporate gifts, fund-raising, or educational purposes. Special editions can also be created to specifications. For details, contact the Special Sales Department, Skyhorse Publishing, 307 West 36th Street, 11th Floor, New York, NY 10018 or info@skyhorsepublishing.com.

Skyhorse® and Skyhorse Publishing® are registered trademarks of Skyhorse Publishing, Inc.®, a Delaware corporation.

Visit our website at www.skyhorsepublishing.com.

10 9 8 7 6 5 4 3 2 1

Library of Congress Cataloging-in-Publication Data is available on file.

Cover design by Brian Peterson
Cover photo credit: Top, AP Images; bottom photos by Anthony LeDonne

Print ISBN: 978-1-5107-4367-0
Ebook ISBN: 978-1-5107-4371-7

Printed in the United States of America

For Lauren. You know why.

Contents

Introduction

For the longest time, *The Marvelous Mrs. Maisel* was one of those shows everyone kept telling me to watch.

"You gotta watch it. You're a comedian!"

"You'll love it. It's set in New York!"

"Check it out. The first episode has boobs!"

So when my agent asked if I could write a cookbook about the show, I said yes.

And then I watched the first episode.

And then I binged the rest.

And then I rewatched the whole season (especially the first episode) and became a total fan.

And how could I not? The show combines two of my favorite *c* words: cooking and comedy. And if you don't like either of those things, I'll call you my *other* favorite c word (crumpet).

Food plays such an important role in the show. The food's not always kosher—was there really shrimp in the eggrolls? It's not always glamorous—Susie dumping a can of beans in a pot made my heart ache. And it's not always appetizing—"Applesauce and peach slices and mashed potatoes and consommé and hard-boiled eggs, and pureed cauliflower and pudding for dessert. Your teeth will wonder what they're there for." (Charmingly eclectic, indeed.)

But food is always there.

And, if you're anything like me (always hungry), you want some way to not only *watch The Marvelous Mrs. Maisel,* but to eat like its characters eat, too.

So with computer on lap and remote control in hand, I took note of every food and drink item showed on screen, discussed, or otherwise mentioned. At the time of this writing, there's only one season of *The Marvelous Mrs. Maisel* available, which means the number of foods featured on the show could only fill half a cookbook. And try as I might, my editor wouldn't let me fill out the rest with jokes from my stand-up act or pictures of my dog.

To come up with other recipes, I asked: "What else would the characters of this world eat and drink?"

The response I heard was unexpected (I was alone at the time) and went something like "knish, kugel, and kreplach." I found it odd that this voice picked only foods that start with *k*, but, since it was close enough to my favorite *c* words, I let it slide.

And then I tested recipes for everything, from an Amaretto Sour (page 13) to the Zagnut (page 192), and have the newly formed love handles to prove it. Many, like The Brisket (page 142),

required several iterations before getting right. Others I nailed on the first try but they still required multiple rounds because they tasted sooo good (hello, Chocolate Almond Cake! page 178).

I ended up with a book full of fresh takes on beloved classics from the culinary world of Manhattan in the 1950s, incorporating modern ingredients and techniques, something the ever-improving Marvelous Mrs. Maisel would approve of.

A Note on Equipment
Bed and Bath is enough, no one needs Beyond.

A comedian doesn't need much for her job—a microphone, a stool, ideally an audience.

Nor does a cook.

I'm amazed at the number of useless gadgets marketed to home cooks.

I've never once said, "I wish had a contraption that slices eggs and only eggs, and only in one-quarter-inch slices," or "hey, Wife, can you pass me that thing that only peels garlic and has no other use in the kitchen?" or "I'm on my twelfth avocado of the day, I wish I hadn't loaned out my avocado peeler!"

One knife does all these things.

I live in a one-bedroom apartment in a Manhattan high-rise. It's barely 600 square feet. My wife, dog, and I hardly fit in here (we each have our own shelf). How am I supposed to fit all those gadgets?

My tiny apartment forces me to keep only the essentials. Everything you see below is in my kitchen. And there's not much more than what's listed. I do have a sous vide water circulator and an industrial-strength blowtorch in my kitchen, but you won't need those for this book.

Between you, me, and the millions of other people who've purchased this book, I often fantasize about having all my worldly possessions stolen, freeing me to rebuild my stuff from square one. I love living clutter free, but it's easier to start from scratch than to get rid of stuff I already own. (I'm still mad I loaned out my avocado peeler!)

You can cook almost all the recipes in this book with the items on the list below.

So, what do you need?

- **A good chef's knife.** Keep it sharp. The sharper the knife, the safer it is.
- **A good cutting board.** John Boos is best. Make sure it's wood. Never get plastic. Plastic will dull your knife faster than you can say "is this thing on?"
- **A good paring knife.** For cutting small things, hulling strawberries.
- **An enameled Dutch oven.** I use Le Creuset.
- **A large skillet.** You don't need fancy stuff. Cast iron is fine. Clean it with soap and water like you would any other pan, and never store it wet or it'll rust. I dry mine on the stove over high heat.
- **A digital scale** that measures in grams and ounces. (More on this later.)
- **A nonstick skillet**, for eggs.

- **A wooden spatula**. The flat surface of a wooden spatula is far superior to a wooden spoon for deglazing a pan.
- **A silicone spatula**. I *love* the bendiness of silicone spatulas. Find one that is sturdy but comes to a sharp edge. This will allow you to mix things better and clean out mixing bowls. (Although, if you ask me, I never minded leaving excess batter in the bowl as a little treat for myself.)
- **Instant thermometer**. Get a Thermapen. It's the last instant thermometer you'll ever buy.
- **Probe thermometer**. This takes the guesswork out of roasts.
- **Fine-mesh sieves** of various sizes. I have three: a small one to double-strain cocktails, a medium one for sauces, and a large one for stocks.
- **Graters**. Microplane is *the* best. I recommend their Professional series without all the plastic as they'll last much longer.
- **A whisk**.
- **Mixing/prep bowls**. I use stainless steel one-cup-sized prep bowls for prepping. All my diced produce goes into these as part of my mise en place (more on that later).
- **A spider,** a.k.a. a spiral wire skimmer. Use these to remove things from cooking liquids, like pasta, matzo balls, or kreplach.

- **Tongs.** For removing larger, studier items from a pan.
- **Tamis.** Two reasons to get a tamis . . . Mashed. Potatoes. It's a tambourine-shaped fine-mesh sieve.

Nice to have, but not required for this book:

- **Electric hand mixer**.
- **Blender**.
- **Food Processer**.

Things you DO NOT need. Ever. Unless you got them as wedding gifts. Like I did.

- Measuring cups. (More on this later.)
- Measuring spoons. (More on this later.)
- A colander. (Just get a spider.)
- Stand mixer. (Unless you bake a lot.)

Bar Equipment

- **A mixing glass**. You can find fancy mixing glasses for a reasonable price at online retailers or traditional brick-and-mortar stores. Use this for any drinks that don't require egg white.

- **A shaker**. Use this for drinks with egg white (Amaretto Sour, page 13, Whiskey Sour, page 27).
- **A barspoon**. Used for stirring drinks.
- **Channel knife**. Not 100% necessary, but handy if you want to make curly twists. You can use a vegetable peeler or a paring knife if you don't need the curly kind.
- **A jigger.** For measuring spirits. My favorite is the double-sided jigger with graduated marks denoting ¼, ½ and 1 ounce on one side, and ⅓, ¾, and 1½ ounce on the other.

A Note on Weighing Things

I developed every recipe using the weight measurements listed but also include volumetric measurements so I wouldn't scare off anyone.

If you take nothing else out of this book, take this: get a digital scale. For the price of two lattes, you can make your cooking tasks much easier, faster, and more consistent.

Measuring stuff with a measuring cup is a pain in the tuchus. You have to get the ingredient into a measuring cup, level it off, and pour it into a mixing bowl. If you're measuring molasses, you've just wasted the better part of an afternoon. And there's all that stuff left inside the cup! You might use the back of a butter knife to scoop out the stuff, or one of those tiny spatulas that makes you feel like a giant ogre (just me?). Or you might throw the measuring cup in the sink to deal with it later. But what if you also need a cup of flour and forgot to measure the dry stuff before the wet? Oy.

If you're like me and Midge, you're always looking for ways to improve.

In this case, you need a digital scale.

What if, instead of measuring a cup of molasses, washing it out, and then measuring a cup of flour, you could just dump both ingredients directly into the mixing bowl?

Sounds pretty good, right? (Say yes.)

Set the mixing bowl on the scale. Tare it (zero it out), then add the first ingredient. Tare the scale again, then add the next ingredient. Repeat until you're so thankful you can't contain yourself and have to DM me on Instagram. (You're welcome in advance.)

It saves you time *and* it cuts down on cleaning. What's not to like about that?!?

Working Clean

I'm a stand-up comedian, and my act is pretty clean on stage. I don't cuss. I'm not vulgar. Working clean saves me from ever having to change my act if I perform on TV, at a church, or in front of my in-laws.

I don't work clean because I have something against cusswords. I cuss when I please and believe the f-bomb is a great way to get a point across. But I am pretty clean when I first meet someone. I'm usually on my best behavior. It's not an act, but it's a toned-down version of me. I

want to feel them out first. See what they're all about. If they're game for fun conversation, then I'll let loose with the f-bombs. But if they're tentative, I'll hold back, and will eventually move onto a more fun conversation. And when I'm doing stand-up, it's almost always in front of people I've never met.

Bottom line: it makes my life easier to work clean.

The same goes in the kitchen. I meticulously clean. Annoyingly clean. Like *clean-the-counters-before-I-start-cooking* clean.

And then I prepare every ingredient first. I don't start cooking anything until every ingredient is lined up in a little bowl, waiting to be used. It's a technique called mise en place (French for "get your shit together"). Once the food is prepped, I wash and dry my knife and cutting board and give the counters a quick once-over to make sure no stray chive (another great *c* word!) is mocking me.

Working clean removes distractions. I'm less likely to bump into things. Which means I can more easily enjoy a glass of wine (or several) while cooking. If my workspace isn't clean, my head isn't clean. My grandma always used to tell me: "a tidy bed, a tidy mind." And I always say: "a tidy counter, a full wineglass." You get the idea, right?

Cooking and Comedy: The Similarities

A comedian refers to her jokes as material. A chef's material? Recipes. When a comedian writes new material, she cuts, refines, and improves—which is coincidentally what a chef does when he creates a new recipe.

A comedian's only responsibility is to see funny things in the world and convince an audience to also think it's funny. Hopefully they think it's funny. And hopefully they all realize this at the same time.

How do we do this?

We speak truths. I mean, we make up everything. But the only way an audience is going to laugh at our jokes is if the jokes hint at something we agree on. Something true.

Which is why I'm not going sugarcoat things in this book (unless the recipe calls for a sugar coating). Nor will I mince words. Unless, of course, "words" happens to be an ingredient that requires mincing. Okay, you know what? All these cooking double entendres are getting out of hand. I was thinking they'd just be a flash in the pan.

Who is this guy?

I'm a comedian (like Midge) who lives in New York City (also like Midge). I even live in her same neighborhood, albeit sixty years in the future. What else do we have in common? We love to entertain and we love to cook (and we both look stunning in a pink dress).

There are some differences. I don't measure myself every day. I don't have kids. And I'm not Jewish. The first difference is unimportant. I need only look at my abs (love handles) to see what

kind of shape I'm in. The second is immaterial for the sake of this cookbook (a random poll of no one tells that raising kids is a cinch). The third, however, requires some explanation.

Had my last name been Ledonowitz instead of LeDonne, these recipes would have been different. I'd have asked my family for recipes. I'd have grown up with these foods. But as a gentile, I had to research. I looked at what people ate during the 1950s. I looked into what Jewish households would have served. I tried putting everything in Jell-O molds.

I don't know what Jewish families eat on the regular. Do they always have bagels? (Yes, according to one Jewish coworker.) Do they always keep kosher? (No, because bacon.)

I also don't know the ins and outs of keeping kosher, and my recipes reflect that. Some have meat and cheese in the same dish, which, based on my conversations with random Jewish people on the street, is not kosher. Also not kosher? Approaching random people on the street and saying, "Are you Jewish?" These recipes aren't guaranteed kosher because I don't know kosher, and it's disrespectful to say "I think this is kosher?" and then totally screw it up. I also think that folks keeping kosher would know far better than me whether something is kosher and be much better equipped to substitute kosher ingredients.

While we're on the topic of recipes, I'll say this: these recipes are inspired by *The Marvelous Mrs. Maisel* world, but they're not directly from it. These recipes are not traditionally Jewish, nor are they traditionally straight from the 1950s. Why? Because the food in the 1950s was different. Life in the 1950s was different. I've put my personal spin on many of them.

If you're looking for traditional recipes, there are tons of cookbooks out there. If you're looking for a fun way to participate in *The Marvelous Mrs. Maisel*, then this book is for you.

Two-Drink Minimum
(Cocktails)

A Note: Cocktail Garnishes

Just as no one worth their margarita salt left her home without a hat in the 1950s, you shouldn't make a cocktail without its garnish. It's like a little hat for the drink, a finishing touch, something to tie an outfit together. But garnishes aren't just pretty to look at; they also serve a purpose—namely to make the drink taste and smell better. Maybe they're more like a hat *and* perfume.

There are three different tools you can use to make a twist.

- First, the channel knife. This is that weird little contraption with a plastic handle and a little metal eyelet. To make a twist, you press the eyelet into the citrus and pull. It'll cut a channel in the citrus rind, and out comes your little twist. Then you can wrap it around a straw or a barspoon to give it a curly shape. Fancy, but fussy.
- Second, the vegetable peeler. This is self-explanatory. Create a peel from top to bottom of the citrus. Do this directly above the drink you're about to garnish, as the flavorful oils will spray out when you peel the citrus. Then gently squeeze the peel over the drink to express the oils toss the peel into the drink. I like to stir the drink with the peel for added flair, but that's up to you.
- Third, the paring knife. I prefer this to the peeler method because when you use the knife, you'll invariably cut some of the pith with the peel. That pith gives the peel a stronger backbone, allowing you to express even more oils when you squeeze it over the drink. (And by now you know I'm all about the oils.)

This all may seem like much ado about nothing, but I'm telling you, I've done my research (I'm half in the bag as I type this) and garnishes make a difference. (Hiccup.)

Homemade Syrups

Simple Syrup

YIELD: ABOUT 1½ CUPS

1 cup (250 g) sugar
1 scant cup (250 g) water

Put sugar and water into a heatproof glass container. Microwave on high until it starts to boil (usually about 5 minutes in my microwave). Stir to dissolve all the sugar. Transfer to a container with a lid (I use mason jars), cool to room temperature, and refrigerate. I recommend using a two-cup Pyrex measuring glass because the handle won't be hot when you pull that boiling mixture out of the microwave.

You don't have a Pyrex measuring glass handy? And you also don't want to pull a piping-hot container out of the microwave? Do it on the stovetop!

Just put the sugar and water in a small saucepan, heat it over medium-high, and remove from heat once it boils. Ta-da! You just saved yourself the $12 it costs to buy the stuff. This book pays for itself!

Mint Simple Syrup

YIELD: ABOUT 1½ CUPS

1 scant cup (250 g) granulated sugar
1 cup (250 g) water
4 cups, packed (60 g) mint leaves

Put sugar and water into a heatproof glass container. Microwave on high until it starts to boil (usually about 5 minutes in my microwave). Stir to dissolve all the sugar. Transfer to a container with a lid (I use mason jars), add mint, and cool to room temperature. Strain the simple syrup into a plastic squeeze bottle or another mason jar and refrigerate. Discard the used mint.

The Amaretto Sour

When Midge and Joel first met, she was drinking an Amaretto Sour. Joel was impressed with her but not her drink—perhaps a foreshadowing of their future trouble in paradise?

A classic member of the sour family, which includes the Sidecar (page 31), the Daiquiri (page 14), and the Margarita (page 21), the Amaretto Sour is a fantastic cocktail. Amaretto takes the place of cognac, rum, and tequila, respectively. But Amaretto is much sweeter. This version tempers the sweetness with a whiskey backbone, a choice I think Midge would enjoy. I don't know about you, but I'd pay good money to have a Palmer Witherspoon following me around 24/7 to refresh my drink.

1½ ounce (45 mL) bourbon, such as High West American Prairie Bourbon
1 ounce (30 mL) amaretto, such as Luxardo
1 ounce (30 mL) freshly squeezed lemon juice
1 egg white

Add all ingredients to a shaker without ice and shake. This may seem ridiculous, but it helps emulsify the egg white so it froths better in the final drink.

Add ice to the shaker.

Shake for at least 30 seconds.

Strain into a chilled cocktail glass and garnish with a lemon twist if you have one available. And you *should* have one available after all that explaining I did in the Cocktail Garnishes section (page 10).

The Daiquiri

YIELD: 1 COCKTAIL

Everyone needs an Imogene in their life. Someone to sip cocktails and chat with while you measure your body every day for ten years. (What are friends for?)

I don't know how Midge makes her daiquiris, but I'm pretty sure Imogene would love my version. You can make these in batches if you're serving a large group or for yourself if you've had a terrible set. I've made batches up to twenty-four hours in advance without any noticeable degradation of the lime.

Do yourself a favor and make your own simple syrup. It's so easy—if you can mix and microwave two ingredients, you can make simple syrup—and will save you from having to buy the expensive stuff in the store.

2 ounces (60 mL) rum (I *love* El Dorado 3 year.)
3/4 ounce (20 mL) freshly squeezed lime juice
1/2 ounce (15 mL) Simple Syrup (see page 11)

Add all ingredients to a mixing glass, jar, cup, or tin filled with ice.

Shake or stir for at least 30 seconds.

Strain into a cocktail glass and garnish with a lime slice.

The Gin & Tonic

YIELD: 1 COCKTAIL

Ah, the G and T. The quintessential summer sipper. Season 2 sees the Weissmans head to the Catskills, a summertime retreat for many in New York during that time.

I highly recommend using good-quality gin and tonic. For gin, I love the citrus, spice, and Italian juniper The Walter Collective uses. Malfy also makes a fun gin. But use whatever you've got. As I always say, the best gin is whichever gin's in your hand. For tonic, Fever Tree makes an excellent option. It's more expensive than the large plastic bottles of tonic, but I'd rather take a page out of Midge's notebook: better, not more.

1 lemon, sliced into ¼-inch-thick wheels
2¼ ounces (70 mL) good gin
4 ounces (120 mL) good-quality tonic

Heat a small skillet or grill pan over medium-high heat. Once it's hot, place the lemon wheels in the pan and brown. Flip once to brown the other side. Set aside.

Fill a double old-fashioned glass with ice. Add gin. Pour in tonic. Give it a gentle stir. Garnish with a sprig of rosemary and the reserved lemon wheel.

For bonus points, after you add the gin, put a barspoon into the glass and pour the tonic down the spoon. It's a fun party trick, and you can taste the extra playfulness.

The Manhattan

YIELD: 1 COCKTAIL

Next to the Martini, the Manhattan is the epitome of classic cocktails.

Made with ingredients sourced from around the world—American bourbon or rye, French sweet vermouth, and Trinidadian bitters—the Manhattan, like Manhattan, is truly a global cocktail. Which is perfect, considering that season 2 of *The Marvelous Mrs. Maisel* sees Midge in Paris.

If you've tried Manhattans before and thought they were too strong, I think you'll like this recipe. It's closer to the original recipe in terms of size and strength. It's bracing enough to remind you it's a cocktail, but it's not so spirited that you'll hop on a train, head to the Village, and get on stage to try stand-up for the first time.

Because the proportion of sweet vermouth is higher in this recipe, use decent stuff. I'll never say no to Noilly Prat. Dolin is delightful. Carpano is cool, too.

---

2 ounces (60 mL) good bourbon or rye, such as
   High West American Prairie or Rendezvous Rye
3/4 ounces (20 mL) sweet vermouth, such as Noilly Prat
2 dashes aromatic bitters, such as Angostura
Amarena or maraschino cherry, for garnish

Add all ingredients to a mixing tin or glass full of ice.

Stir for 60 seconds. Don't shake this drink. Every time you shake a Manhattan the Monopoly Man loses his monocle.

Strain into a chilled cocktail glass and garnish with an Amarena or maraschino Cherry. (Luxardo makes a fantastic maraschino cherry, available on Amazon.com.)

The Margarita

YIELD: 1 COCKTAIL

Another cousin to the Whiskey Sour (page 27), the Daiquiri (page 14), and the Amaretto Sour (page 13), the Margarita would be equally welcome at the Copacabana or at the Maisel's while entertaining guests.

2¼ ounces (70 mL) tequila
1 ounce (30 mL) Cointreau
1 ounce (30 mL) freshly squeezed lime juice
Kosher salt, for rim
Lime wedge, for garnish

Remember that lime you *just* squeezed for this? Save the pressed lime half and rub its still slightly juicy wetness on the lip of your glass. (That was a little explicit; must have been reading one of my wife's romance novels today . . .) Dip the moistened lip (there I go again) of the glass into a small saucer covered with ⅛ of an inch of kosher salt.

Add the rest of the ingredients and ice to the glass and stir. Garnish with a lime wedge.

The Martini

YIELD: 1 COCKTAIL

Calling cocktails "martinis" is like calling all comedians Lenny Bruce. Sure, we'd all like to be him, but there can be only one.

A Martini contains *only* gin and dry vermouth (orange bitters is optional) and is garnished with olives or a lemon twist. Never vodka (that's called a Kangaroo). Never onions (Gibson).

And if you like it "bone dry, like Winston Churchill liked it," you're really just drinking chilled gin (and I judge you).

Making a Martini can be intimidating. A drink with so few ingredients leaves no room for error. Over-pour, under dilute, stare too long at your guests with your mouth gaping and you're asking for trouble (and a lot of uncomfortable guests).

Some people will (ridiculously) claim that shaking bruises the gin. They are wrong. Shaking accelerates dilution. Shaking drinks that contain sugary ingredients can lead to cloudy cocktails. They'll look disgusting, but they won't taste any different.

———

2¼ ounces (70 mL) good gin, such as The Walter Collective (my personal favorite)
¾ ounce (20 mL) dry vermouth, such as Noilly Prat
1 dash of orange bitters (optional), such as Angostura

Put all ingredients in a glass with ice. Any glass will do.

Stir for 60 seconds. (I don't need to explain how to do this, do I?)

Strain into a chilled cocktail glass. I use a julep strainer and think you should too. You could use two forks, as I've suggested before. The goal, once again, is to separate ice from the liquid.

Garnish with an olive or two. Your other alternative is a lemon twist. Not a slice, a wheel, or wedge. A twist. (See page 10 if you want to know more about why I'm adamant this should be a twist and nothing else.)

The Negroni

YIELD: 1 COCKTAIL

Ahhhh, the Negroni. I love this drink. It's so bitter and Italian (just like me).

It has equal parts gin, Campari, and sweet vermouth. No OJ, no bitters, and everything is in equal parts. But bartenders mess it up all the time. I have no idea how or why; the recipe is on the back of the friggen Campari bottle!

I've had bartenders make up stories about how this is a "riff on a Manhattan" (it's not) and that's why they have used gin, sweet vermouth, and bitters.

Or that it's "just a gin martini with a splash of Campari."

I could see Harry Drake ordering this at the Friars Club before Susie's inevitable assault. Or any of the patrons at the Copacabana. It makes for a wonderful *aperitivo* before dinner.

1 ounce (30 mL) gin
1 ounce (30 mL) Campari
1 ounce (30 mL) sweet vermouth

You can serve these "on the rocks" or "up." If you prefer on the rocks, fill a double old-fashioned glass with ice, pour in the ingredients, give it a quick stir, and garnish with an orange twist.

If you'd like it up, follow these steps:

Put all ingredients in a glass with ice. Sure, you can use a fancy crystal mixing glass, but you can also use a pint glass. Or any glass. Hell, you could use a plastic jug for all I care. The whole point here is to chill and ever-so-slightly water down the cocktail.

Stir for 30 to 60 seconds. (I don't need to explain how to do this.)

Strain into a chilled cocktail glass. I use a julep strainer. You can use two forks. The goal is to separate ice from the liquid. Get creative.

Continued on page 26

Garnish with an orange twist. (Not a slice, a wheel, or wedge. And definitely not lemon. A twist can be as simple as taking a vegetable peeler or knife and peeling off a strip of orange peel, and then expressing the oils into the drink. If "expressing" is too fancy for you, then replace it with "squeezing." This is NOT just for decoration. The oils in the peel are flavorful and aromatic and complement the drink nicely.)

Notes

- Every time you use a craft gin in a Negroni, a hipster's beard grows an inch. Craft gins are too flavorful and not dry enough for a Negroni. Plus, they're way too expensive for mixed drinks. Gordon's, Beefeater, and Tanqueray are fine.
- Don't use anything else except Campari. And don't you dare use Aperol. If any bartender tells you Aperol is a more approachable Campari, punch him in the waistcoat. They are owned by the same company but are different. Campari is 24% abv, Aperol is 14%. Campari is bitter. Aperol tastes like watermelons.
- The sweet vermouth is where you can be fancy. Carpano's Antica Formula is my favorite. I also like Punt e Mes but only use half as much because it's sweeter. Noilly Prat and Dolin are fantastic. Cinzano Martini & Rossi, and the other less-glamourous vermouths are fine here too.

The Whiskey Sour

Whoever named the whiskey sour gets zero points for originality. Other drinks have fancy names: The Martini, The Manhattan, The Slippery Nipple. But the whiskey sour? It sounds exactly how it tastes. What the name doesn't convey is that there's a balanced sweetness to make this cocktail more than just a zesty zap of citrus.

2 ounces (60 mL) bourbon (I love High West American Prairie Bourbon)
¼ ounce (5 mL) Simple Syrup (page 11), or Mint Simple Syrup (page 11)
½ ounce (15 mL) freshly squeezed lemon juice
1 egg white (optional)

Add all to a shaker without ice and shake. This may seem ridiculous, but it helps emulsify the egg white so it froths better in the final drink. Add ice to the shaker and *now* you may shake for at least 30 seconds. Strain into a chilled cocktail glass and garnish with a lemon twist.

The Old-Fashioned

YIELD: 1 COCKTAIL

The Old-Fashioned is the little black dress of cocktails. It's timeless, classic—it looks damn good on just about everyone.

There are many ways to make an Old-Fashioned. Most of them are terrible. If you're muddling fruit, you're doing it wrong. If you're pouring without measuring, you're doing it wrong. If you're using anything but a base spirit, a bit of sugar, and ice, you're doing it wrong. Keep it simple, and more refined, by following the recipe below. And just like a little black dress is at its best with the perfect accessory, don't even think about serving an Old-Fashioned without its garnish.

2 ounces (60 mL) good bourbon or rye, such as High West Distillery American Prairie Bourbon or Rendezvous Rye
½ ounce (15 mL) Simple Syrup (page 11)
2 dashes aromatic bitters, such as Angostura

Add all ingredients to a mixing glass full of ice.

Stir for 60 seconds.

Strain into a double old-fashioned glass filled with ice or one large ice cube or sphere. Garnish with an orange twist—not a wheel, wedge, or any other shape. Just a twist. A good Amarena or maraschino cherry would be acceptable as well.

You could use Mint Simple Syrup (page 11) in this cocktail for a nice twist! For a fun riff, you can also try aged rums and tequilas and other bitters.

The Sidecar

YIELD: 1 COCKTAIL

The first time I tried cognac, the bottom of my mouth went completely numb.

It was late in the evening. I was working (drinking) with a batch of nearly newly minted consultants from around the world at our company's training camp (not a joke) an hour outside of Chicago. One of these people was from France. He loved cognac and wanted me to love it too.

I did not.

Until that point, I had been cognac-free, and after that point, I decided, I would remain cognac-free.

But then a few years passed. And the other, more terrible tasting spirits I'd experimented with (grappa) burned off enough taste buds that by the time I accidentally tried cognac again, I liked it. A lot. Not as much as Susie loves whiskey at the Kettle of Fish bar, but it was far better than I remembered.

---

2 ounces (60 mL) good cognac
½ ounce (15 mL) Cointreau
½ ounce (15 mL) freshly squeezed (not pre-squeezed or bottled!) lemon juice
¼ ounce (5 mL) Simple Syrup (page 11)

A Note on Cognac:
Don't waste XO in a cocktail, but use decent cognac, such as VSOP. Any brand mentioned in a rap song will suffice.

Add all ingredients to a mixing tin or pint glass full of ice. (Any container will do. Get something clean that'll hold liquid and put all the ingredients in there. This isn't rocket science.)

Stir for at least 30 to 60 seconds. Use this time to tell a joke. They're a captive audience and they want what you've got. They'll laugh. Yes, you can shake the drink, and some people will tell you that you *have* to because it has citrus (you don't), but shaking this drink makes it cloudy, and cloudy drinks are not sexy.

Strain into a chilled cocktail glass and garnish with an orange twist. Do not cut an orange wedge or wheel or any other shape. Just. A. Twist.

The Vesper

YIELD: 1 COCKTAIL

Vesper, in Latin, means *evening*, which happens to be the best time to drink this particular cocktail. How coincidental that its name is also its prime drinking time? (Those Latins were on to something.)

This is the drink that put James Bond on the map. Or maybe I have it backward (I do). Maybe I've had a few of these with my muse and am now fully inspired (hammered). Doesn't matter. The point is, this drink is fantastic.

The Vesper doesn't appear in *The Marvelous Mrs. Maisel*. But James Bond started fighting villains around the same time that Midge started telling jokes. That's a good enough reason to include it in this book, no? Pour one for Maisel, Miriam Maisel.

1¼ ounces (40 mL) good gin (I love The Walter Collective gin)
1¼ ounces (40 mL) good vodka (The Walter Collective also makes a flavorful vodka)
½ ounce (15 mL) Lillet Blanc

Add all ingredients to a mixing glass, jar, cup, or tin filled with ice.

Shake or stir for at least 30 seconds.

Strain into a chilled cocktail glass and garnish with a lemon twist.

Opening Acts
(Starters)

Baked Brie, Phyllo, and Onion Jam

YIELD: 6–8 SERVINGS

This dish doesn't appear in *The Marvelous Mrs. Maisel* world, but I think it would be right at home for a Weissman or Maisel dinner party. It's classic upscale Midge, a great way to fancy up casual get-togethers, or to eat all by yourself with a nice glass of Chardonnay, Sancerre, or Champagne when the going gets tough. It looks fancy, but, between you and me, I think it's easy enough for even a shorthand girl like Penny Pann to figure out.

1 (9-ounce) wheel of Brie
¼ cup Onion Jam (recipe follows)
8 sheets of phyllo dough, thawed
6 ounces butter (85 g), melted
3 tablespoons (10 g) thyme
⅓ cup (50 g) seedless red grapes, cut in half, sprinkled with sea salt

Preheat the oven to 400°F.

Cut the brie wheel in half lengthwise, like a bagel you're getting ready to schmear. Slather half of the onion jam between the two halves and reassemble. Set aside.

Place two sheets of phyllo dough on a work surface. Overlap them so that they make a square. Paint the sheets with melted butter. Place two more sheets over the first two. Paint with butter. Repeat with the remaining sheets.

Place the Brie wheel in the center, slather the top of the wheel with the remaining onion jam. Sprinkle thyme like it's raining herbs. Pull the corners together and pinch it at the top. You could do something fancy here . . . or just smoosh it together like I do.

Transfer to a parchment paper lined–baking sheet. Bake for 15 minutes. Serve with grapes or anything else you desire.

Onion Jam

YIELD: ¼ CUP

1 tablespoons (14 g) butter
1 tablespoons (10 g) olive oil
½ pound (226 g) onions, ½-inch dice
1 tablespoon (15 g) brown sugar
¼ teaspoon (1 g) kosher salt
4 tablespoons (60 g) balsamic vinegar (don't waste D.O.P. balsamic here; I.G.P. is fine!)
3 tablespoons (10 g) thyme

Add the butter and olive oil to a sauté pan and melt over medium heat.

Add onions, reduce heat to medium-low, and cook until caramelized, about 45 to 60 minutes. Add a few tablespoons of water if the onions get too dry. Adjust the heat so they don't fry. You're looking for more a translucent brown color, not a fried brown.

Add the brown sugar, salt, balsamic vinegar, and thyme to the onions and reduce to a syrup.

Deviled Eggs

YIELD: 16 FILLED EGG HALVES

The Weissmans prepared hard-boiled eggs for the Mordecai Glickman surprise guest dinner, but they could have easily substituted Deviled Eggs. They're fun to eat and fun to say! I don't know what makes them deviled—there's only a sprinkling of harissa powder to give them a red tint, and they're not spicy—but who am I to argue with tradition?

I've taken these deviled eggs up a notch and given them the lox bagel treatment. The olives and capers give a nice pop of flavor and help cut through the luxurious fat while the red onion gives a nice pop of crunch. Oh, and those capers? They become something totally different after a quick dip in hot oil.

8 eggs
4 ounces (113 g) cream cheese
1½ tablespoons (20 g) good mayonnaise, such as Hellman's
½ cup (40 g) olives, diced
1 teaspoon (4 g) kosher salt, divided
115 grams yolks from eggs
vegetable oil, as needed
¼ cup (30 g) nonpareil capers
¼ cup (50 g) red onion, sliced
2 tablespoons freshly squeezed lemon juice
1–2 tablespoons chives, cut into ½-inch-long pieces

Bring a pot of water to a boil. Remove from heat, add all 8 eggs, cover, and let sit for 20 minutes. Remove to an ice bath and let cool for 30 minutes. Peel and cut eat egg in half along its long axis. Remove the yolks to a large bowl. Set the empty halves to the side.

Continued on page 41

Add the cream cheese, mayonnaise, olives, and half of the salt to the egg yolks and mix thoroughly. Put the schmear into a small ziplock bag. Seal the bag and snip off a small part of one of the corners. Set aside.

Use a sieve to drain the capers. Dry them on a paper towel–lined plate.

Heat 1 inch of vegetable oil to 375°F in a small saucepan over medium heat. Working in batches, carefully add capers to oil and fry until they split open and get crispy, about 45 seconds. Use a fine-mesh sieve to remove them from the oil and set them on a fresh paper towel–lined plate.

In a small bowl, place the sliced onion, lemon juice, and the remaining salt. Let pickle for 10 to 15 minutes.

In the meantime, divide the egg yolk mixture evenly among the egg whites, squeezing it out through the hole you cut in the ziplock bag. Top each egg with a few capers, a few slices of pickled red onion, and a few chive pieces.

French Onion Dip

Yield: 4–6 servings

While this dip isn't featured on the show, I have a pretty good feeling it would be in Rose's rotation of party foods (that Zelda would prepare, of course).

This dip is really good. So good, in fact, that my wife and I may have finished off an entire bowl in one sitting while I was writing this cookbook. It's not too creamy since the onions make up a good proportion of the contents. The secret here is to make sure the dip is nice and *moist*. (I realize I just made 98 percent of you uncomfortable.) I find this dip to be heavier than others, so use a sturdier chip or cracker. I can say from experience that Ritz crackers work well (see note about Wife and me slamming the entire bowl).

Caramelization takes a long time. Like an-hour-or-longer long. But it's not active time. Once you start cooking the onions, you've got plenty of time to work on anything else. So sit back, relax, and have yourself a few cocktails while those babies get sweet, sweet caramel brown.

2 tablespoons (28 g) butter

2 pounds onions (900g or 5-6 cups), ½-inch dice

1 tablespoon Better Than Bouillon

4 tablespoons dry white wine

3 tablespoons (10 g) fresh thyme

4 ounces (114 g) Gruyère

6 ounces (170 g) crème fraîche (or sour cream)

6 ounces (170 g) good mayonnaise, such as Hellman's

Add the butter and onions to a large sauté pan and sweat over medium-low heat until the onions caramelize, about 60 minutes, stirring occasionally to caramelize evenly. If the onions get too dry, add a few tablespoons of water and stir. You're not trying to brown the onions; you're trying to caramelize them. If they start browning, turn the heat to low. You should hear a gentle sizzling but nothing more than that.

Add the bouillon, white wine, and thyme to the pan. Turn heat up to medium and reduce the liquid to a glaze. Once you achieve the glaze, move the onions to a bowl.

Add the Gruyère, crème fraîche (or sour cream), and mayonnaise to the bowl with the onions and mix thoroughly to combine.

Gougères

*Yield: About **20** Gougères*

Rose Weissman describes gougères to Shirley Maisel as "French cheese puffs." I think that's about as accurate and concise as you can get.

These are perfect finger foods for cocktail parties, dinner parties, or when your wife's out of town and you don't want to guzzle those martinis on an empty stomach. I love having a bowl of these when guests first arrive, as we're all huddling around the kitchen counter while I pour champagne. You can make them earlier in the day and put them in the oven 20 minutes before your guests arrive.

3½ ounces (100 g) butter
1 cup (250 g) water
1⅓ cups (200 g) flour
4 eggs
⅔ cups (50 g) Cheddar cheese

Add butter to a small saucepan and melt over medium heat. Add water, heat to a simmer.

Add flour to the saucepan, increase heat to medium-high, and stir constantly. You want it hot enough to cook out some of the flour flavor but not too hot that it starts browning. Reduce the heat if it starts browning.

Once it comes together into a doughy ball and stops sticking to the sides of the pan, remove from heat and let cool for 5 minutes.

Add one egg, stir to fully incorporate. Add the remaining eggs, one at a time, stirring to fully incorporate.

Preheat the oven to 400°F.

Scoop balls the size of Ping-Pong balls onto a parchment paper–lined baking sheet, top each ball with a bit of cheese, and bake for 20 minutes, or until golden brown.

Gravlax

*YIELD: **4–6** SERVINGS*

I love lox. Any lox. Gravlax. Belly lox. Goldilocks.

But I grew up hating it. It's how I was raised. I'm from the Pacific Northwest. We have 482 kinds of salmon, and we're taught to thumb our noses at East Coast salmon. We have coho, Chinook, and Copper River salmon, which is only in season for two days every third spring and retails for $800 per pound.

They have Atlantic. Plain old Atlantic salmon.

My parents raised me to hate Atlantic salmon. Their parents raised them to hate Atlantic salmon. (My grandparents learned it from the Native Americans.)

But then I moved to New York. I put my prejudices aside and tried Atlantic salmon. And it was delicious. To my West Coast family and friends: give Atlantic salmon a try. I think you'll be surprised.

Put this on a bialy, blini, or bagel. (Anything that begins with a b.)

---

4 tablespoons + ½ teaspoon (50 g) kosher salt
3 tablespoons (40 g) sugar
½ cup (20 g) fresh dill, chopped
1 ounce gin (optional)
1 pound (453 g) center-cut salmon fillet, pinbones removed

Mix salt, sugar, dill, and gin in a bowl and set aside.

Cut a piece of plastic wrap about one-and-a-half times longer than the fillet and place it on your work surface. Place the salmon on plastic wrap, skin-side down. Sprinkle the salt mixture over the salmon, pressing it into the flesh. Wrap the fish in the plastic wrap and place it on a small baking sheet.

Continued on page 48

Place another baking sheet on top of the fish and weigh it down with whatever you have handy—a few cans of beans, that jar of gefilte fish from Astrid, or the giant mezuzahs, also from Astrid.

Refrigerate for 2 days.

Rinse off salt and sugar and pat dry with paper towels. If you prefer a firmer texture, refrigerate it for 12 to 24 hours, uncovered.

To serve, slice thinly with a sharp knife and serve with bagels and schmear or some rye bread.

Mixed Nuts, following page.

Mixed Nuts

YIELD: *6* CUPS (ABOUT *12* SERVINGS)

While Midge is busy doing some top-notch honing at Mary's party, Susie's finally understanding why people go to parties instead of buying some Sno Balls and a beer and taking the subway at rush hour: the food table. She starts in on the lobster, finishes the clams, and has Midge pass her some asparagus. (Did anyone else not expect her to eat green things? Just me?) What we didn't see—but what Mary probably set out in various locations—were mixed nuts. No party is complete without mixed nuts.

This recipe boils (bakes?) down to two steps: mix, bake. I like to prep the tray of nuts and pop it into the oven about 20 minutes before my guests arrive. That way the first thing my guests smell when they arrive is my rosemary-scented mixed nuts.

¼ cup (15 g) fresh rosemary, leaves removed from stems, finely chopped
6 cups assorted unsalted raw mixed nuts, such as walnuts, almonds, pecans, brazil nuts,
¼ cup good olive oil
1–2 teaspoons kosher salt
1 teaspoon Maldon sea salt
½ teaspoon cayenne pepper

Preheat oven to 350°F.

If you're unfamiliar with removing rosemary leaves from its stem, follow these steps. Pinch the rosemary about a ½ inch from the top. Use your other hand to run your fingers from top to bottom, stripping off the leaves.

Add all ingredients to a large bowl and toss to combine.

Place nuts on a foil-lined baking sheet and spread out in one even layer. Bake until nuts are browned and fragrant, about 10 minutes. Give them a stir halfway through to ensure they brown on all sides. Let them cool for 5 minutes before serving.

Moroccan Cigars

YIELD: *20* CIGARS

Smoke 'em if you've got 'em!

These are Moroccan cigars. We don't see them on the show, but they could have easily been served at the Miriam's wedding. (Just don't tell the rabbi about the cheese and butter, which is just as unkosher as the shrimp egg rolls.)

4 tablespoons (40 g) canola or olive oil
1½ pounds ground beef (you can substitute any other
     ground meat, such as lamb or turkey)
2½ cups (350 g) onions
1 package phyllo dough
½ cup (100 g) grated provolone, or another soft cheese,
     such as mozzarella or cheddar
4 tablespoons (60 g) butter, melted

Brown the meat. Add 2 tablespoons (20 g) of the oil to a large skillet set over high heat. Working in batches, brown the ground beef. Once browned, scoop out the ground beef and place in a sieve set over a bowl. Discard the fat. Set the ground beef aside.

Sauté the onions. We want around 2 tablespoons (20 g) of fat in the pan for the onions. If there's any residual fat left in the pan from the ground beef, leave it. If there's more than 2 tablespoons, spoon it out. If there's less, add a little oil. Set the pan over medium-high heat. Add the onions and sauté. This step moves rather fast. Stir or toss the onions to make sure they don't burn. Once they're brown, remove from the pan and mix with the meat. Set aside.

Place a large piece of parchment paper on your counter. This is your work surface. Unroll 1 sheet of phyllo dough and place on the work surface. Cut in half lengthwise (the long way). Put a flatware tablespoon–sized scoop of the meat and onion one inch from one end.

Continued on page 52

Put a generous sprinkle (around 2 tablespoons) of cheese on top of the meat and roll into the shape of a cigar. Use a paintbrush to paint the outside with butter. Transfer to a parchment paper–lined baking sheet.

Repeat until all the meat/onion mixture and phyllo are used or you've gotten so frustrated with the phyllo dough you've thrown it at the wall.

Preheat the oven to 350°F. Bake for 30 minutes or until well browned.

A Note on Phyllo Dough

I've been using phyllo dough since I was a kid—for some reason, I was obsessed with baklava from an early age. Despite using phyllo that long, I still cuss and get frustrated when the dough doesn't behave exactly as I want it to.

First, remember to defrost your phyllo dough. You don't want to get ready to cook this recipe and then have all your plans derailed because you forgot to read the directions on the package. (Why are they so small!?! They should be in giant red letters! Why am I starting these 2 minutes before guests arrive?) There are two ways to defrost it: put it in the fridge overnight, or put it on the counter for two hours. Either way, if you're making these for a get-together and procrastinate as much as I do (I finished this book moments before you picked it up), you don't want to be caught with your phyllo down.

Second, phyllo is fragile. Be gentle with it. Pretend they're pages from an ancient scroll (Leviticus). Imagine you're an archaeologist. Imagine you just discovered them in a cave with a giant rolling ball and poisonous darts. Imagine you have a whip. The point is: be gentle. (Side note, where can one buy a whip?)

Third, keep it moist. Here's another place to follow the directions on the package. Cover the stack with plastic wrap and a damp towel. This stuff dries out fast. And the drier it is, the more fragile it becomes. You don't want the pages to tear before you escape the temple of doom. (And just like that, we're back to the Indiana Jones references.)

Shrimp in the Egg Rolls!

YIELD: 10–12 EGG ROLLS

The Marvelous Mrs. Maisel opens with a bang—or rather, a splash—as Midge announces to the attendees that yes, there is shrimp in the egg rolls. This isn't cause for alarm for a lot of people—save those with shellfish allergies, in which case, wow, Midge, shouldn't you have disclosed the clandestine crustacean beforehand?—but for those keeping kosher, this is not good. Papa and the rabbi have a brief discussion. The news cascades into a cacophony of kvetching. And we are hooked on a brand-new show.

1 pound shrimp, 12–15 count, peeled, deveined, and thawed (optional)
2 tablespoons (25 g) olive oil
1 teaspoon kosher salt
2 tablespoons (25 g) canola oil, plus more as needed if frying
3 green onions, white and green parts, 1/8-inch-slice
2 cloves garlic, minced
1 cup carrots, shredded
2 teaspoons fresh ginger, minced
3 cups napa cabbage, 1/4-inch-slice
2 tablespoons soy sauce
1 package spring roll shells

Cook shrimp. Preheat the oven to 425°F. Gently toss the shrimp with olive oil and salt. Place shrimp in one layer on a foil-lined baking sheet. Roast for 8 to 10 minutes, or until lightly browned. Another way to tell when the shrimp are done is when they curl into a soft *c* shape. Pull them out before they curl into a tight, almost circular *c* or they'll be overcooked and will taste like rubber. Remove from the oven and let cool. Cut into ¼-inch dice and set aside.

Sauté veggies. Add 2 tablespoons canola oil to a 10-inch skillet and warm over medium-high heat. Add green onions, garlic, carrots, ginger, and cabbage. Sauté, stirring frequently, until lightly

Continued on page 54

browned, about 5 minutes. Add the soy sauce and reduce to a glaze, 1 to 2 minutes. Remove vegetables to a bowl and set aside.

Assemble. Place one shrimp's worth (estimate, also, optional) of shrimp on a spring roll wrapper, about an inch from one of the corners. Add 2 tablespoons of veggies. Fold the corner over the contents, fold each of the two side corners inward, then roll it up.

If frying, heat ⅛ inch of canola oil in a large skillet over medium heat. Once it shimmers, add a few egg rolls and fry until browned, turning once each side is browned, about 8 minutes.

If baking, heat oven to 425°F. Place the egg rolls on a foil-lined baking sheet, brush with canola oil, and bake until golden brown, about 15 minutes.

If shallow frying, fill a small saucepan halfway with canola oil and set over medium-high heat. Once the oil reaches 375°F on a candy thermometer, add egg rolls in batches, probably only two to three at a time, and cook until browned, about 2 minutes. Use a spider to remove from oil and let cool on a paper towel–lined plate.

That's Gold! Million-Dollar Dip

YIELD: 4–8 SERVINGS

"That's Gold, Jerry! Gold!"—Kenny Bania, *Seinfeld*

That's the first thing I said after making this dip. The only thing, actually, since after that my mouth was full. Also, I'd made things awkward because it was just me and my wife.

In the dip world, this is total gold. It's good to have in your repertoire. You can throw it together in a few minutes and let it chill in the fridge while you get ready for your guests to arrive. It's great for football parties. Cocktail parties. Any party, really. Including cocktail hour with your spouse, which is how I came to devour it.

This dip is my take on the classic from Neiman Marcus, but let's just pretend it's from B. Altman's as-yet-unseen cafe.

This goes great with champagne, gougères (page 45), and fabulous company.

You can omit the bacon if it's not your cup of tea.

¼ cup (2 ounces, 50 g) slivered almonds
4 slices (25 g) bacon
8 ounces (225 g) cheddar
½ cup (20 g) green onions, ¼-inch slices
4 ounces (100 g) sour cream
4 ounces (100 g) good mayonnaise, such as Hellman's
4 ounces (100 g) crème fraîche
1 (.53-ounce, or 15 g) French onion dip packet

Continued on page 57

Add the almonds to a medium skillet over medium heat. They'll start smelling nutty when they're toasted. Once finished, transfer to a small bowl. Set aside.

Put bacon on a metal cooling rack on a foil-lined baking sheet. Put in a cold oven. Turn on the oven to 400°F. Cook until bacon is crispy, about 20 minutes. Set aside.

Mix the cheese, green onions, sour cream, mayonnaise, crème fraîche, and the French onion dip packet together in a large bowl. Add the bacon and slivered almonds. Cover with plastic wrap and refrigerate until ready to serve.

Crème fraîche is fancy sour cream. Give it a shot. Its flavor is more interesting than regular sour cream. If you want to go crazy, replace the sour cream with crème fraîche, as well. Whatever you do, please don't use reduced-fat anything for this recipe. I realize people are trying to be health conscious, but you won't get the full effect. If I may offer another suggestion, instead of going with reduced fat, just have less? I know, I know, you probably want to punch me. But look at it this way: Midge would rather have better, not more.

White Bean Dip

When I think of the 1950s, I think of cocktail parties. It could be because I'm drinking an Amaretto Sour (page 13) and listening to Frank Sinatra and Count Basie. . . . Every cocktail party needs food. And in case you couldn't tell from this book, there's no easier party food than dip. Make this a day ahead to give yourself more time to cocktail with your guests.

1 cup dry (200 g) cannellini beans
4 cup (1000 g) water
4 (30 g) cloves garlic
2 tablespoons (6 g) lemon juice
2 tablespoons (5 g) thyme
½ teaspoon salt + more based on taste
1 cup reserved cooking liquid
Flat-leaf parsley, as needed (optional)
Pine nuts, as needed (optional)
Harissa powder, as needed (optional)

Add beans and water to a saucepan and bring to a boil. Reduce heat to maintain a simmer and cook until the beans are tender. Don't test one bean and call it good! Some of them may cook faster than others. Sample at least 4 or 5 beans before making the call.

Use a fine-mesh sieve to strain the beans and reserve 1 cup of the cooking liquid.

Add the beans, garlic, lemon juice, thyme, and salt to a blender and blend until smooth. The dip should have the texture of toothpaste. Add the reserved cooking water to thin the dip as necessary. Taste, and season with more salt if needed.

To serve, transfer dip to a wide bowl. Make a well in the center of the dip and garnish with 2 to 4 tablespoons of really good olive oil. Garnish with chopped parsley, pine nuts, and a few shakes of harissa powder.

Leek Fritters

YIELD: *7–10 FRITTERS*

I don't exactly know who in *The Marvelous Mrs. Maisel* world would make these, but I wanted to include them because they are so flavorful. They're like a vegetable version of a latke.

I picture the fortune teller telling Rose about this recipe in between reading tea leaves and giving her a charm to help Midge keep her husband.

2 tablespoons (28 g) butter
5 cups (325 g, about 3 – 4) leeks, white and light green parts
½ cup (40 g) panko
1 egg + 1 egg white
2 teaspoons (8 g) salt
canola oil, as needed

Add butter to a nonstick skillet over medium heat. Add the leeks. Lower the heat to medium-low and cook until caramelized, about 45 minutes. Remove leeks from pan and set aside.

Mix the panko, egg, egg white, and salt in a small bowl. Mix together with the leeks.

Add canola oil to a nonstick skillet set over medium heat. Spoon a mound of leek mixture into the pan. Fry until browned, about 2 to 3 minutes per side.

Transfer to a paper towel–lined plate. Serve garnished with sliced green onion and crème fraîche.

Challah French Toast

YIELD: 2 SERVINGS

I love everything French. Their fries, their toast, their kissing.

I haven't been to France, but I can't wait to go and eat French toast every morning. When in Rome and all that. I don't know what they call regular toast, but I don't care. Give me French toast or give me death! (Also, the kissing.)

French toast always seemed extravagant to me. And so sweet with all that maple syrup (from Canada, a French-speaking country, even!). It seems like a special-occasion breakfast. I picture Midge making this for Joel on Valentine's Day, or maybe for Papa on Father's Day. Or maybe for herself after a late night at the comedy club. The addition of vanilla bean and nutmeg makes it taste sweeter than it actually is. You can substitute ¼ teaspoon pure vanilla extract for the vanilla bean pod, but it won't taste as rich. If you can't find challah, substitute brioche.

5 extra-large eggs
½ teaspoon (2 g) kosher salt
½ vanilla bean
1½ teaspoon (1.5 g) freshly grated nutmeg
2 challah rolls, sliced 1 inch thick, lengthwise
4 tablespoons good butter, such as Kerrygold

For serving:
Good maple syrup (Grade C is more flavorful than Grade A, strangely enough)
Peanut butter, warmed slightly to make it easier to spread
Butter (my favorite! Note: either salted or unsalted is fine here.)
Pinch of Maldon sea salt (I love the sweet-salty combination of maple syrup and sea salt.)

Crack eggs into a small bowl. Add the salt. Beat with a fork until there are no longer any large globs of egg white visible. You want a homogeneous mixture.

Continued on page 64

Use a paring knife to cut a whole vanilla bean in half. Cut across the width of the bean. Reserve the other half for another use. Make a slice down the length of the remaining vanilla bean half, being careful not to cut all the way through the bean. Use the tip of the paring knife to pry back the sides of the bean along the cut you just made, exposing the seeds. Run the blade of your knife down the length of the pod, scraping out the tiny seeds. Add the seeds to the eggs.

Grate nutmeg into egg mixture, a little less than one half of a nutmeg seed for two servings, and beat to combine.

Pour egg mixture onto a large plate or casserole dish and add the challah roll slices. Soak for 10 minutes, turning the bread over after 5 minutes.

Heat a large sauté pan over medium. Add butter.

Add soaked slices to pan containing butter and fry until lightly browned, about 4 to 5 minutes. Reduce the heat to low, flip each slice, and cook for an additional 4 to 5 minutes.

Move the slices to two plates, with the browner side facing up. Top with butter, melted peanut butter, maple syrup, or Mint Simple Syrup (page 11). Or go wild and make your own combination of all the above!

Tea with Sophie Lennon

YIELD: 12 SCONES

We all have moments where we feel like a fish out of water. Maybe we're somewhere we don't think we belong (living with our parents). Or we're somewhere we know we shouldn't be (lying in bed waiting for our friends to text to cancel plans because all we want to do is order a pizza and binge-watch *The Marvelous Mrs. Maisel*).

However, we get there, and we all hope we handle it with the same aplomb as Midge when she visits the famous Sophie Lennon. And we all hope we leave with a brand-new fur coat.

Chive and Cheddar Scones

YIELD: 12 SCONES

"I would never eat a domestic scone."—Midge.

Just in case your shipment of scones isn't as fresh as usual—and thank goodness your version of Dawes sampled everything, as manservants are so talented at doing—I've supplied this recipe for you.

I'm not generally a sweets guy (that's a lie). I'm more of a savory fella (I eat everything), so I made these without any sugar. If you like your scones a little sweeter, feel free to add three to four tablespoons of sugar in the first step.

2¼ cups (300 g) flour
2 scant teaspoons (8 g) baking powder
½ teaspoon (1.5 g) baking soda
1¼ teaspoons (5 g) kosher salt
9 tablespoons (130 g) butter, diced into ½-inch pieces
5 tablespoons (70 g) cream
7 tablespoons (90 g) crème fraîche
2 cups (150 g) cheddar cheese
½ cup (40 g) chives

Continued on page 67

Use a whisk to mix together the flour, baking powder, baking soda, and kosher salt in a large bowl. Add the butter. Use a hand mixer or a stand mixer fitted with the paddle attachment and, on its lowest setting, mix the butter until all the large pieces are broken up.

Add the cream and crème fraîche and mix. Again, use the lowest setting so the cream doesn't go flying out of the bowl. Add the cheese and chives, and stir to combine.

Turn the dough out onto a piece of parchment paper. Squish it together to form a ball. Place another piece of parchment paper on top and roll to a rectangle roughly ½ inch thick. We use the parchment paper instead of flour so we don't have to use extra flour. Extra flour changes the recipe and makes a mess.

Cover the rectangle in plastic wrap and refrigerate for at least 2 hours.

Cut the dough into rectangles 2 inches by 4 inches and place them on a parchment paper–lined baking sheet. Cover with plastic wrap and freeze for at least two hours.

Preheat the oven to 325°F. Remove the plastic wrap and bake for 20 minutes, or until golden brown on top. (No need to defrost.)

Serve with Clotted Cream (recipe follows), jam, or really good butter.

Clotted Cream

Yield: 2 cups

1 quart heavy cream

Pour the cream into a large casserole dish. Put it into the oven and set it for 170°F, or as low as it'll go. Bake for 12 hours. It will develop a thick golden skin. This is normal. Remove the dish from the oven, cover with plastic wrap, and cool to room temperature. Then refrigerate for at least 8 hours. Gently peel back one of the corners of the golden skin to expose the thin liquid beneath. Decant that liquid. Scoop the golden goodness on top and the creamy stuff right below it into a bowl and refrigerate until ready to use.

Finger Sandwiches

High Tea with Sophie Lennon is about as fancy as tea can get. Bread for the finger sandwiches and the macarons (NOT macaroons) are from France. The clotted cream and scones are from London. Even the lemon arrives on a silver tray.

Have Dawes whip these up while you're getting out of your fat suit.

Isn't that marvelous?

———·····———

The Sophie Lennon: Spread good mayonnaise (such as Hellman's) on white bread. Sandwich with presliced American cheese and a slice of bologna. Wrap in newspaper, stuff into a rucksack, and jiggle around in your fat suit.

The Real Sophie Lennon: Cut a lemon into four wedges. Suck on the wedge. Dab your mouth with a fine linen napkin. Hand the lemon rind and the napkin to Dawes. Look at all the other sandwiches with judgment.

Midge in Paris: Spread European butter (such as Kerrygold or Plugra) on ½-inch-thick baguette slices. Sandwich with a slice of *jambon* and another slice of baguette. If *jambon* is unavailable, substitute with prosciutto di parma (for a more Italian version) or good ol' American ham (for a more American version).

Late-Night Midge (Meatloaf-Tomato): Spread butter on two slices of sourdough bread. Spread a teaspoon of tomato paste on top of the butter. Sandwich with a slice of leftover Midge's Meatloaf (page 155) trimmed to fit the bread. Trim the crusts and cut into pieces.

Gruyère-Onion Jam: Spread mayonnaise on two slices of white bread. Spread Onion Jam (page 38) on one side. Top with thinly sliced gruyere. Trim crusts and cut into pieces.

The Hausfrau from Queens (grilled cheese): Spread mayonnaise on two slices of white bread, on what will be the outside of the sandwich (it'll help with browning). Sandwich with two slices of presliced American cheese. Add 2 tablespoons butter to a nonstick skillet over medium heat. Add the sandwich and brown both sides, about 2 minutes per side. Trim crusts and cut into pieces.

The Dawes (grilled cheese): Use white cheddar instead of American cheese, and sourdough instead of white bread. And sandwich with plenty of leftover caramelized onions (page 84).

The Astrid (Smoked Whitefish): Toast two slices of rye bread. Spread mayo on one slice, sour cream on the other. Sandwich with smoked whitefish, fresh dill, and sliced celery. Trim the crusts and cut into pieces.

Camembert-Pear: Toast challah slices and cut into square pieces. Spread with Camembert cheese. Top with sliced pears and leftover Candied Harissa Almonds (page 73).

One-Liners
(Soups, Sandwiches & Salads)

Salads

Arugula with Orange, Olives, and Harissa-Candied Almonds | 73

Chickpea and Olive Salad | 75

Smoked Whitefish Salad | 76

Tabbouleh | 77

Watermelon Salad with Feta, Mint, Olive Oil, and Harissa | 81

Sandwiches

Vivian's Egg Salad Sandwich | 83

Half Chopped Liver on Challah | 84

Salmon (Bagel) Sandwich | 87

Soups

Borscht | 88

Chicken Stock | 90

Goulash | 93

Kreplach Dough | 95

Kreplach Filling: Mushrooms & Thyme | 97

Kreplach Filling: Roast Chicken & Smoked Gouda | 98

Matzo Ball Soup | 99

Arugula with Orange, Olives, and Harissa-Candied Almonds

SERVES 4–6

We've all been in a position where we thought an elderly person your dad works with was coming over, but it turned out to be a lawyer our dad wanted to us to hire so we could divorce our estranged spouse, right?

Anyone?

When the Weissmans think Mordecai Glickman is coming over (rest in peace), they prepare a half-dozen dishes that require little chewing. When they realize their mistake, Rose, Miriam, and Zelda spring into action to cook some other, more textured, dishes, but they come up empty handed.

This salad would have bought Zelda some much-needed time to defrost the steaks. It looks fancy and takes almost no work at all. In a pinch, you can drop the candied almonds, which should allow you to make this dish in five minutes flat.

The recipe for candied nuts makes more than you'll need for the salad, but do not make less than prescribed. You will snack on these as they cool. And you will burn your mouth several times. You'll eat so many you won't have enough for the salad itself and will have to make another batch. (Ask me how I know . . .)

Continued on page 74

Dressing:
2 tablespoons lemon juice
6 tablespoons olive oil
2 pinches of kosher salt

Salad:
1 orange
1 grapefruit
1 pound (453 g) arugula
1 cup (120 g) pitted kalamata olives, halved lengthwise

Harissa-Candied Almonds:
1 cup (150 g) raw almonds
1 teaspoon (3 g) harissa powder
1 tablespoon (14 g) butter
¼ cup (75 g) sugar
1 teaspoon (3 g) salt

To make the dressing, whisk the lemon juice, olive oil, and 2 pinches of kosher salt together in a small bowl. Set aside. (Yes, I know you should add the olive oil in a slow drizzle while constantly whisking to ensure it's emulsified, but here's a confession: I've never tasted a difference. Seriously. I've never once eaten a salad and screamed to the waiter, "EXCUSE ME! The dressing isn't fully emulsified. Take this back.")

Use a chef's knife to cut off the top and bottom of the orange. Then, going from top to bottom, cut away the peel and the pith (the white stuff) on the sides.

Hold the orange in your hand and use a paring knife to cut into one of the segments, cutting along the connective membrane. Cut to the center of the orange but no further. Repeat on the other side of the segment, then scoop out the segment. Repeat with all the other segments. Set aside.

Repeat these steps with the grapefruit. Set aside.

Add the almonds, harissa, butter, sugar, and 1 teaspoon of salt to a medium-sized skillet over medium heat and stir to mix together. Once the sugar melts, stir to coat the nuts and to ensure the mixture doesn't burn. Transfer the candied nuts to a parchment paper–lined baking sheet or a bowl. Once they've cooled, break them apart and set aside.

Add the dressing to a bowl. Add the arugula and stir to combine. Divide among 4 to 6 serving bowls and top with citrus segments, olives, and nuts.

Chickpea and Olive Salad

YIELD: 4 SERVINGS

The Weissmans eat salad more than a few times during the first season. Their tastes generally lean toward a simple lettuce salad—which surely has more to do with Zelda's laziness than the fact that it's a prop—but I think they'd welcome a change. Should Rose ever ask me for a suggestion, I'd offer this salad. I think it would be as equally welcome on the Weissmans' table as Ethan is in front of the TV (or as the daughter is to being written out of the script).

3 tablespoons olive oil
2 teaspoons fresh squeezed lemon juice
1 can chickpeas, rinsed
1 cup kalamata olives
1 English cucumber, ½-inch dice
3 tablespoons red onion, ¼-inch dice
¼ cup flat-leaf parsley
½ cup feta

Whisk together the olive oil and lemon juice in a large bowl. Add all the ingredients and toss to combine.

Smoked Whitefish Salad

YIELD: *4–8 SERVINGS*

No one's ever eaten tuna fish salad and thought "What's better than this?" (Because the answer is "anything.")

But if they did, smoked whitefish salad would be the answer. The texture is more delicate, and less stringy. The flavor is fresher, slightly smoky, and goes really well with brunch mimosas.

1 red onion
3 tablespoons + 1 teaspoon freshly squeezed lemon juice, divided
1 tablespoon olive oil
½ cup plain yogurt
4 tablespoons (10 g) fresh dill, chopped
Kosher salt
2 heads of butterhead lettuce
16 ounces smoked whitefish, meat removed from bones and broken into pieces
Cucumber, thinly sliced

Pickle the onions
Cut the red onion in half and peel. Cut each half into ¼-inch slices. Transfer to a bowl and add 3 tablespoons lemon juice. Toss to combine. Set aside for 15 minutes, stirring once or twice.

Prepare the dressing
Whisk olive oil and remaining lemon juice together in a small bowl. Add yogurt and dill and stir to combine. Season with salt. Reserve.

To complete
Dress the salad only right before serving. Add dressing to a large mixing bowl. Add lettuce and toss to dress. Divide among 4 plates for a lunch-sized portion, or 8 plates for an appetizer-sized portion. Top with cucumber, smoked whitefish, the reserved dressing, and pickled onions.

Tabbouleh

YIELD: 4–6 SERVINGS

When we first meet Astrid, Midge's sister-in-law and recent convert, we learn that while she is overzealous, she's also earnest. It's not inconceivable that she would have had tabbouleh on one of her eleven trips to Israel.

I'm including a version of it here because it's a wonderful side dish for any of the recipes in the Mains section. This also makes for a great lunch to bring to work. It's healthy, is easy enough to make ahead, and has no crazy smells that would annoy coworkers.

3/4 oz (20 g) + 1 tablespoon (14 g) olive oil
1 cup (200 g) uncooked quinoa
2 cups (475 g) Chicken Stock (page 90) or water
2 teaspoons (8 g) kosher salt
2 bunches (2 cups packed; 50 g) parsley leaves
4 large sprigs (½ cup packed; 5 g) mint
½ bunch (¼ cup packed; 15 g) green onion
1 cup (150 g) cherry tomatoes
1½ tablespoons (20 g) fresh squeezed lemon juice
¼ cup (30 g) pistachios

Heat 1 tablespoon of oil in a small saucepan over medium-high heat and add quinoa. It will start to smell toasty and you'll hear little pops. That's the quinoa celebrating getting toasted. Mazel tov! Cook, stirring frequently, until lightly browned, about 3 to 5 minutes.

Add the chicken stock or water and the kosher salt to the quinoa and bring to a boil. Once boiling, remove from the heat, cover, and let sit until all the liquid has been absorbed, about 15 minutes. If there's still liquid remaining after 15 minutes, return to low heat until it's evaporated. Let cool completely.

Continued on page 79

Rough chop the parsley. Your parsley should only be leaves, no stem. The stems are just tasteless filler, like most of my jokes. Ditch them.

Chiffonade the mint. To chiffonade, stack the mint leaves, roll them like a cigar, and then slice them in the same direction you were just rolling. You'll end up with thin ribbons. So fancy!

Slice the dark green part of the green onion on a severe bias. The bias just makes for a more interesting shape—long spades instead of rings—so if you're not feeling up to it, just cut rings. Slice the cherry tomatoes in half. Toss together in a large bowl. Set aside.

Juice the lemon. Measure 1½ tablespoons of lemon juice and add it to a small bowl. Save the rest for another use.

Add the rest of the olive oil and whisk to incorporate. Don't worry about adding an emulsifier (mustard, soap, etc.) here. It's a rustic salad.

Mix the quinoa into the greens. If you're making this in advance, pause here until you're ready to serve. When you're ready to serve, add the dressing to the salad and toss to coat. Taste the salad; it probably needs more salt. Add pistachios, and toss again, you tosser, you!

Feel free to riff on this recipe. Shred any leftovers from the Roast Chicken (page 160) and toss in the salad. Try chickpeas, almonds, feta, whatever you'd like!

Watermelon Salad with Feta, Mint, Olive Oil, and Harissa

YIELD: 4 SERVINGS

How beautiful is this salad! So good. So pink. So salady. But not too salady. Almost no green stuff, save for a few leaves of mint and pistachios, if you can count those. Use the ripest watermelon you can. The melon should feel heavy for its size and should sound hollow.

1 pound (453 g) watermelon, 1-inch cubes
a heaping ½ cup (100 g) feta cheese
⅓ cup (40 g) pistachios
2 tablespoons (25 g) olive oil
Kosher salt, to taste
¼ cup mint
1 tablespoon harissa powder
8 tablespoons parsley

Add all ingredients to a large bowl and mix to combine. Divide among 4 serving bowls. Garnish with parsley.

Vivian's Egg Salad Sandwich

Yield: 3 sandwiches

Every office has that one coworker who can't *not* bring eggs to work. Maybe it's the guy trying to lose weight by only eating hard-boiled eggs (and telling everyone about it). Or maybe it's that gal who hasn't had a conversation that didn't include the word *keto* in two years. B. Altman has Vivian.

I love Vivian. So happy. So smiley. I was sad and a little angry when someone took her egg salad sandwich. Who does that? (Mary.)

I wanted to give her a replacement, but I wanted to take it up a notch.

This version of egg salad is my wife's favorite. The addition of truffle oil gives it just a hint of elegance that egg salads so often lack.

5 eggs
¼ cups + 2 tablespoons (75 g) good
   mayonnaise
½ teaspoon black truffle oil

¼ teaspoon (1 g) kosher salt
3 tablespoons chives
6 slices of bread, such as regular white bread

Prepare an ice bath. Fill a bowl with ice and add water so the ice can swim freely.

Hard-boil the eggs. Put the eggs into a small saucepan, cover with water, and turn the heat to high. Once it reaches a boil, remove from heat, cover, and wait 12 minutes. Use a skimmer, or spider, or whatever it's called, to gently remove the eggs from the saucepan and place them in the ice bath until completely cooled, about 10 minutes.

Peel the eggs under running water and dry them with a paper towel. Add all the eggs to a bowl, add all the other ingredients, and break up the eggs with a fork. Alternatively, you can use a ricer or potato masher to break up the eggs.

Divide the egg salad mixture among three pairs of bread slices. Feel free to toast your bread if you prefer a crunchy complement to the egg salad.

Half Chopped Liver on Challah

"What am I, chopped liver?"—Chopped Liver

Liver gets a bad rap. I don't know why. It's so flavorful. So sweet. So livery. It's a staple on Jewish deli menus.

2 hard-boiled eggs
1 (453 g) pound chicken livers
4 tablespoons (50 g) schmaltz, canola oil, or olive oil, plus more as needed
1 pound (453 g) onions, ¼-inch dice
2 cups (3½ ounces or 100 g) arugula or watercress
2 challah rolls, or 4 slices of challah bread

Hard-boil and peel the eggs. Reserve.

Season the chicken livers with salt. Add oil to pan over medium-high heat. When oil shimmers, add livers. Cook until browned but still a little pink inside, about 2 to 3 minutes per side. Pull one out and cut it open to test for doneness. Remove the livers from the pan and set on a paper towel–lined plate.

Add the onions to the pan and reduce heat to medium-low until well caramelized, about 60 minutes. Adjust the heat so the onions don't brown too quickly. Remove from the pan and cool to room temperature.

Mix everything together and puree until smooth in a food processor. You're aiming for a spreadable texture, somewhere between wet sand and toothpaste. Add canola oil or olive oil as necessary to achieve the right texture.

Cut the rolls in half lengthwise. Toast the challah rolls or bread.

Divide the liver mixture and the arugula between the 2 challah rolls or 4 slices of challah bread.

Salmon (Bagel) Sandwich

Yield: 2 sandwiches

The is a great before-work breakfast, midday snack, or late-night nosh after killing (or bombing) for 20 minutes at the Gaslight. If I were Midge, I'd keep my refrigerator and pantry stocked with these ingredients to celebrate a good set, or to comfort Joel after he bombs.

2 bagels, halved, your choice of flavor (plain, sesame, everything . . .
   but pick blueberry and prepare for my judgment)
red onion, as needed, about 3 slices
4 ounces (114 g) cream cheese
4 tablespoons (30 g) nonpareil capers
6 ounces (170 g) of salmon gravlax (page 46)

Spread the cream cheese on the bagels. Pro tip: add the capers and onions now. Cementing them in the cream cheese will prevent them from rolling around while you're trying to eat the sandwich.

Roll the salmon pieces and place them on the sandwich. Rolling the salmon will give it more texture, and it'll feel less like you're trying to saw through slippery salmon layers.

Borscht

YIELD: **4–6** SERVINGS

Based on the trailer, which, at the time of this writing, is the only clue about the happenings in the sophomore season, season 2 finds Midge and the Weissmans heading to the Catskills, a.k.a. the Borscht Belt.

And what better tie-in to the show than to make the dish that bears the same name?

For this recipe, you'll need a blender. To achieve a silky, velvety texture, always blend longer than you think.

2 pounds (900 g) beets, washed, greens removed
2 cloves garlic, peeled, lightly crushed
1¼ cups (300 g) plain yogurt
1¼ cups (400 g) sour cream
¼ cup (10 g) dill
2 tablespoons (6 g) freshly squeezed lemon juice
Kosher salt, to taste
Cracked pepper, to taste
Cucumber (optional), diced

For the croutons:
4 tablespoons (50 g) chicken fat, canola oil, or olive oil
4 slices rye bread, cubed

Bring a large saucepan of salted water to a boil, add beets, and reduce to a simmer. Cook until the beets are tender, about 45 to 75 minutes, depending on the size of your beets. They are done when you can pierce them with a paring knife with no resistance.

Use a spider or slotted spoon to remove the beets to a bowl and let cool. Add garlic to the cooking liquid and simmer for 10 minutes. Use a spider to remove the garlic and reserve. Strain the cooking liquid through a fine-mesh sieve and reserve.

Peel the beets. I find it easiest to use a paper towel to rub the skin off the beets, but a paring knife also works.

Add the beets, yogurt, sour cream, dill, lemon juice, and salt to a blender and blend on high until smooth. Blend for longer than you think. If the liquid is too thick, add some of the reserved cooking liquid a few tablespoons at a time. Taste the soup in the blender and add more salt as necessary. Don't add extra salt before getting the texture right, as the reserved cooking liquid is already seasoned. If you didn't read this step all the way through and have already added extra salt and still need to adjust the texture, add plain water to adjust the texture.

Move the soup to a storage container, cover, and refrigerate overnight.

For the croutons

Add oil to a large skillet and set over medium heat. When the oil is fragrant, add rye bread cubes, turning them as needed to brown it on all sides. Adjust the heat so it doesn't burn. Remove to a paper towel–lined plate.

To complete

Divide the soup among 4 to 6 bowls. Add a few croutons, a few pieces of diced cucumber, a few sprigs of dill, and a few sprinkles of cracked pepper. Garnish with a few dots of good olive oil (or just a glug) and a small quenelle of crème fraîche or, if you're sick of me using crème fraîche, a tablespoon of sour cream.

Chicken Stock

YIELD: ABOUT 4 CUPS

Homemade chicken stock is always better than store-bought. And it's quite easy to make.

I make chicken stock in a pressure cooker. Pressure cookers were much more common in the 1950s, so it's not too far-fetched to assume the Weissmans owned one. Zelda would have prepared it, of course. I've listed both preparation methods below.

You'll note that this preparation is much simpler than many other recipes. That is intentional. I find it easier to make a basic stock with chicken carcasses without all the additional vegetables and then just add them as needed when preparing a dish. Often times, I'll just use this stock as-is without any additional vegetable flavoring. I've never once thought "Where is that faint, almost nonexistent carrot flavor?" If you prefer a bit more flavor, you can add chopped aromatic vegetables. A few carrots, onions, celery stalks, and garlic cloves wouldn't be unwelcome here.

1 chicken carcass (perhaps the remains from the Roast Chicken, page 98)
12 cups (3000 g or 3 L) water

Stockpot method: Add the chicken and water to a large stockpot over high heat. Bring to a boil and adjust heat to maintain a light simmer until reduced to 4 cups (1 liter), about 3 hours.

Strain and reserve the stock. Discard the chicken remains.

Pressure cooker method: Reduce water to 4 cups (1 liter) and cook on high pressure for 2 and a half hours.

Goulash

Yield: 4 servings

"Goulash is a dish that suits all ages."—Rose Weissman

I agree, Rose. This dish will warm the bellies and spirits of people young and old during winter. It's hearty, but healthy, with a generous serving of paprika to give it a punch of flavor. You can use smoked paprika here for additional flavor.

1 pound (453 g) beef, cut into 1-inch cubes
Kosher salt, as needed
2 tablespoons (25 g) olive oil
2 cups dry red wine
2 cups beef stock

1 pound potatoes, 1-inch cubes
1 pound carrots, 1-inch pieces
1 pound onions, quartered
¼ cup paprika

Salt the meat on all sides. Add olive oil to a large Dutch oven set over medium-high heat. When the oil begins to shimmer, add the meat. Work in batches to brown the meat on all sides. If you crowd the meat, it will steam rather than brown, resulting in a tougher, more overcooked texture. Use tongs or a spider to transfer the beef to a paper towel–lined plate.

Add the wine to the pan and use a wood spatula to scrape up any brown bits. Reduce the wine until it's a glaze, about 15 minutes.

Preheat the oven to 300°F.

Add the beef stock, paprika, and reserved beef to the pan. Transfer to the oven and cook, covered for 1 hour.

Carefully add the potatoes and carrots to the pan. Don't go splashing that flavorful beef stock all over the place!

Cover and cook for 1 hour. Then add the onions to the pan. Cook, uncovered this time, for 1 more hour.

Kreplach Dough

YIELD: *40 KREPLACH*

This. Is. Kreplachhhhhhh. These are kreplach? Is kreplach plural or singular? Both? The true definition of kreplach may have been lost to antiquity (it hasn't), but the real meaning: delicious.

3 cups (450 g) flour
3 extra large eggs
1 teaspoon salt

Mound the flour in a pile on a clean countertop. It should look like a little mountain. Make a crater in the center as a reservoir for the eggs.

Crack the eggs on a flat surface and pour into a small bowl. Add the salt and beat with a fork until there are no discernible globs of egg white. You want a homogeneous mixture.

Tips

Fill with less filling than you think you should. Maybe a tablespoon total.

The dough will dry out once it's rolled out. Cover it with a damp paper towel or clean dishrag to keep it all moist.

Pour the eggs into the reservoir. Use a fork to stir the eggs and incorporate flour from the top of the crater a little bit at a time. Push up the sides of the flour mound to contain the egg mixture. Don't panic if you have a breach and the egg lava flows down the mountain. Pull some flour from the other side of the flour mountain and push the lava back into the crater. (Are you still with me and my volcano analogy?)

Continue stirring until the egg and flour mixture comes together in one large mass. Use your hands to mix the flour into the eggs. You want the dough sticky but not tacky.

Use the palm of your hand to knead the dough for 5 to 7 minutes. Wrap in plastic wrap and set it in the fridge to relax for at least 30 minutes, or up to 24 hours. You may see some discoloration if you rest it for that long, but that's okay. The oxidation is just on the surface and won't affect the final product.

Continued on page 96

Divide the dough in half and roll each half between two pieces of parchment paper. I find it easier and cleaner than using a cutting board and flour or a counter and flour. Or getting flour everywhere. (Why am I always wearing black when I roll dough?)

If you have a pasta rolling machine, roll the dough until it's thin enough to pass through the machine. If not, then use a rolling pin (and prepare for a full-body workout). Either way, you want to roll this pasta out into paper-thin sheets. Once complete, cut them into 5-inch squares.

Fill with kreplach fillings (recipes follow), fold in half to make a triangle, and pinch all the seams to seal.

Kreplach Filling: Mushrooms & Thyme

The soy sauce will not only season the mushrooms, it'll kick up the umami flavor. And you can never have enough thyme. Thyme's up! Last thyme, I promise! Okay sorry . . . I do this all the thyme.

6 tablespoons (15g, 1 small bunch) thyme
2 tablespoons (25 g) olive oil
1 pound (453 g) mushrooms (such as cremini, trumpet, oyster, etc.), ¼-inch slices
2 tablespoons (40 g) soy sauce
4 tablespoons (50 g) butter

Tie a 6-inch-long piece of kitchen twine around the thyme bunch. This will keep it all in one bundle so that you can more easily remove it when you're done.

Add the olive oil to a medium skillet set over medium-high heat. Add the mushrooms and cook, stirring occasionally, until the mushrooms are browned, about 7 to 10 minutes. You want to brown them, so don't stir too frequently. Stir/toss just enough so they don't burn.

Add the soy sauce to the pan and stir to combine. Continue cooking until most of the liquid has been absorbed or has evaporated.

Reduce heat to medium and add butter and thyme bundle. Cook until butter smells nutty, about 4 to 5 minutes.

Remove from heat, cool to room temperature, and then refrigerate up to 3 or 4 days.

Kreplach Filling: Roast Chicken & Smoked Gouda

I always have one piece of chicken left over from roasting it. I usually shred it and add it to pasta, but enclosing it in kreplach makes for a fun twist. The cheese will melt as the dumpling cooks, making for an ooey gooey surprise. (Don't let me use the phrase *ooey gooey surprise* again.)

¼ pound (114 g) roast chicken (page 160)
¼ pound (114 g) smoked Gouda cheese, shredded
Kosher salt, as needed

Shred the roast chicken into small pieces. Give it a rough chop if necessary to ensure the pieces are quite small, almost a minced texture. Combine with the cheese and a sprinkle of kosher salt to taste. Stuff in kreplach dough.

Matzo Ball Soup

YIELD: *20–23 BALLS, 6–8 SERVINGS*

There seem to be two matzo ball camps: those who like dense balls, and those who like light and airy. This recipe is for dense balls. For airy balls, add ¼ teaspoon baking powder to the dry matzo meal.

4 large (220 g) eggs
1 cup (150 g) matzo meal
¼ cup schmaltz (chicken fat) (50 g) melted (You could use
   the rendered duck fat from the Sautéed Duck Breast [page 163])
¼ cup (65 g) Chicken Stock (page 90), plus (an optional) 3 quarts
1¼ teaspoon (5 g) kosher salt
8 tablespoons (20 g) parsley, thyme, or dill, minced

Note: Some people like their matzo ball soup clear. If that's you, you'll need another quart of chicken stock and you'll have to simmer your balls in a separate saucepan of seasoned chicken stock.

Mix all ingredients together in a large bowl. No, you don't have to beat the eggs, or mix the wet ingredients and dry ingredients separately. As long as you mix everything together thoroughly, your balls will be just fine. While that is generally better practice to ensure proper mixing, I did it both ways and didn't notice a difference.

Chill for 2 hours or overnight. This is important. Matzo needs time to hydrate.

Bring the chicken stock to a gentle simmer in a sauté pan or a wide pot with a lid. Season the stock like you would any other soup. Taste it. It should taste moreish, as in you should want more of it after one sip. I won't specify an amount here because people have different tastes, but if you've read this book from the beginning, by now you know I think most people under-salt everything.

Continued on page 101

If you're in the clear soup camp, warm up the separate stock. Season with salt.

With wet hands, grab about 20 grams' worth of batter and roll into a ball, roughly the size of a golf ball. Plop the ball into the simmering chicken stock and repeat until you're out of batter. I find it easier to rinse my hands between balling so they don't stick to my hands. Simmer for 15 to 20 minutes, or until they're cooked through.

Transfer matzo balls to serving bowls and ladle in clear warmed chicken stock or cooking liquid.

Feature Acts
(Vegetables & Sides)

Susie's Beans

YIELD: 4–6 SERVINGS

I love Susie's practicality. She eats a can of beans right out of the pan she warmed them in. But she deserves better. This dish pays homage to the original recipe (open can, eat) but introduces some variety in the beans and some interest in the flavors. The ingredient list is long, but you've probably got everything except the bell peppers on hand already.

I use Better Than Bouillon and water here instead of chicken stock to keep this simpler, more Susie-ish. I use so much chicken stock at home, I find it's easier to keep a small jar of Better Than Bouillon in the fridge than jars and jars of chick stock.

7 ounces (200 g) bacon
1 (16-oz) can black beans, rinsed
1 (16-oz) can garbanzos, rinsed
1 (16-oz) can cannellini beans, rinsed
3 cups (750 ml or 750 g) water
1 tablespoon Better Than Bouillon, chicken flavor
1 teaspoon (1.5 g) cumin
2 teaspoons (3 g) chili powder
2 teaspoons (3 g) smoked paprika

1 teaspoon (1.5 g) cayenne, optional if you want a kick
1 teaspoon (1.5 g) dried oregano
1½ cups (200 g) red bell pepper, ¼-inch dice
1½ cups (200 g) green bell pepper, ¼-inch dice
crème fraîche, optional
Cheddar cheese, optional
Fritos, optional
Green onion, optional, sliced

Cook the bacon. Place bacon slices on a cooling rack placed on an aluminum foil–lined baking sheet. Put into a cold oven. Set to 400°F and cook until crispy, 20 to 25 minutes.

Add all ingredients except the bell pepper and bacon to a large pot and cook over medium heat until simmering. Reduce heat to low and cook until liquid reduces to the texture of chili, about an hour. Add the diced bell pepper at the end and stir to combine.

Divide among serving bowls and top with crème fraîche, grated cheddar cheese, Fritos, and/or sliced green onion. Or eat them straight out of the pan, like Susie does.

Blini

YIELD: *20 BLINI*

I love potato blini. Everything about them. They look cute. Even the name itself is cute.

Blini. It sounds like a sidekick in a Pixar movie, doesn't it?

Make a bunch of them, and they'll be your little minions. They even kind of look similar.

They're like little clouds on which you can layer different flavors. But whatever you top it with, make sure it's flavorful. A common topper is caviar. Tiny, crunch, salty. I think that's what caviar tastes like. I don't know, I'm not a Russian oil tycoon.

Here we top it with gravlax and deep-fried capers for a rich and salty crunch combo.

These will taste *very* plain on their own, severely lacking in salt. If you find yourself cursing my name, just take a deep breath and remind yourself, "These are supposed to be topped with something salty, like gravlax."

You could easily top these with roasted red peppers for a vegetarian version. Or caramelized onions. Ohh, man, I'm getting hungry again.

1 pound (450 g) Yukon Gold potatoes
4 tablespoons (56 g) butter + more as needed
2 tablespoon (25 g) crème fraîche
2 eggs
2 tablespoons (20 g) flour
Maldon sea salt, as needed

Put potatoes in large pot and cover with at least 1 inch of cold water. Turn the heat to high. Once it comes to a gentle simmer, adjust heat to maintain just a gentle simmer. You don't want a full boil, as it could damage the outsides of the potatoes. (If the outsides get damaged, the potatoes will begin to absorb water, which means they won't absorb as much fat later!)

Continued on page 108

Cook until you can easily pierce the largest potato with a knife. It should slide in smoothly. You shouldn't feel any starchy resistance once they're fully cooked, about 30 minutes. If they're larger, they could take as long as 40 to 50 minutes or longer. Keep that knife handy and, after 20 minutes of simmering, test every 10 minutes.

Drain in a large sieve (or your tamis!) or remove the potatoes from the water with a spider, skimmer, or whatever.

As soon as the potatoes are cool enough to handle, peel them with your fingers.

Meanwhile, put 4 tablespoons of butter and the crème fraîche into a large mixing bowl.

Put the potatoes through a ricer, food mill, or my favorite, a tamis. You can process the potatoes directly into the bowl. If you feel more comfortable handling the tamis, you can place a sheet of parchment paper directly on your countertop and process the potatoes through the tamis right onto that sheet.

If you didn't process the potatoes directly into the bowl, add them to the bowl with 4 tablespoons of butter and the crème fraîche. Use a wooden spoon and mix to incorporate.

Add the eggs one at a time and stir to incorporate. You're going for the texture of pancake batter. Add some of the flour to thicken if necessary.

Heat a medium nonstick skillet over medium low heat. Add a small pat of butter to the pan and swirl the pan to coat. Spoon flatware teaspoon-sized dollops of batter into the pan and cook until browned on one side, about 4 minutes. Flip the blini and cook for until browned on the other side.

Serve with gravlax, caviar, or just a small dab of crème fraîche and a pinch of Maldon sea salt.

Blistered Green Beans

YIELD: 2 SERVINGS

Is anyone else surprised at how many vegetables the Weissmans eat? Don't get me wrong—I'm happy they always have vegetables on the table. It's more than I can say for most Americans (me).

Green beans make an appearance more than once in *The Marvelous Mrs. Maisel*. Many people steam their beans. Which, unless it's for a Nicoise, I find a little boring. I much prefer a little heat treatment for my beans. We're blistering them under the broiler for a few minutes here, so you get that nice roasted flavor in just a few minutes. The slivered almonds provide the crunch, and the feta cheese ties everything together. If you don't have slivered almonds, you can substitute shelled pistachios, peanuts, or lightly crushed walnuts.

Serve this as an easy steak-night side or in larger quantities and at room temperature for a party.

1 pound (453 g) green beans
4 tablespoons (50 g) olive oil
2 teaspoons (8 g) kosher salt
¼ cup (35 g) slivered almonds
¼ cup (40 g) feta

Preheat the oven to 450°F. Arrange green beans in a single layer on an aluminum foil–lined baking sheet. Drizzle olive oil and kosher salt liberally over beans.

Roast for 8 minutes.

Add the almonds to the beans. It's easiest to pull the rack out, add the almonds, and then return the beans to the oven.

Roast for 2 minutes.

Transfer the beans and almonds to a serving bowl and top with the feta cheese.

Butter-Roasted Carrots

YIELD: 4 SERVINGS

Maybe Zelda has the night off. Or you're more focused on a main item, like the Brisket (page 142) or the Rack of Lamb (page 151). Or maybe you just feel like a bunny. Doesn't matter. This dish is easy, tasty, and the pop of color and textures from the parsley, mint, pistachios, and feta make for a nice surprise.

1 pound (453 g) carrots
1 pound (453 g) butter
4 tablespoons (5 g) parsley
8 tablespoons (2.5 g) mint
¼ cup (40 g) feta

¼ cup (30 g) pistachios
Kosher salt, to taste
4 garlic cloves, optional
1 bunch (20 g) thyme, tied with a piece of
    kitchen twine, optional

Wash the carrots, scrubbing vigorously. Wrap a clean dishrag around the carrot and push and pull the carrot through it. Seriously. You're going to be uncomfortable. You're going to make anyone watching you uncomfortable. But when you're done, the carrots should have a soft, velvety skin. Which I think makes this whole exercise even more awkward.

Melt butter in a large sauté pan. You want a pan small enough to fit the carrots, but not so large that you have tons of extra room. I used a 12-inch cast iron skillet. You can chop them into shorter lengths if you wish, but I prefer the presentation of full-length carrots.

Add the carrots to the pan. Careful! Don't splash any of that butter. This is the time to add the optional garlic and thyme.

Preheat the oven to 300°F.

Carefully move the carrots to the oven and roast for 2 hours. If the carrots aren't completely covered in butter, rotate or baste them occasionally so they don't dry out.

Remove from oven. Transfer the carrots to a cooling rack on an aluminum foil–lined baking sheet. Transfer the butter in the pan to a jar. Congrats, you just made carrot-flavored ghee! Use this as you would butter, keeping in mind that it'll have a subtly sweet flavor.

Toss the carrots with parsley, mint, pistachios, feta, and salt (to taste) and serve.

Scalloped Potatoes

YIELD: 6–8 SERVINGS

My grandma used to make scalloped potatoes whenever the whole family got together. If it wasn't on the menu, I'd scream until she added it. (I was an angel.)

This is another dish that wasn't shown on the show but was popular during the 1950s. The Maisels may have even considered it as a side option for their steak night when they met Penny, the shorthand girl, before settling on the mashed potatoes (page 114).

It takes a little bit of work, but the results are worth it, I promise. Just be aware that your guests may scream if you don't have it on the menu the next time they come over.

3 pounds (1.4 kg) russet potatoes
5 cups (1 kg) cream
1 bunch (20 g) of thyme, tied with a piece of
   kitchen twine

1 tablespoon (12 g) kosher salt
5¼ ounces (150 g) cheddar cheese, divided,
   1¾ ounces and 3½ ounces
¼ cup (25 g) panko

Peel the potatoes. Then, working in batches, slice them on a mandoline, dropping the potatoes into a bowl of water immediately after slicing.

Add the cream, the thyme, and the salt to a large saucepan. Add potatoes and bring to a simmer. Adjust heat to simmer for 20 minutes. Drain, reserving both the potatoes and the cream. Discard the thyme.

Preheat the oven to 350°F.

Sprinkle with ⅓ of the cheese and a bit of cream. Add more layers of potatoes and cheese and cream. Try to divide the cheese and cream evenly among the layers, but if you can't, and have leftovers, it's okay. I won't judge you. Just add it all now.

Mix the remaining cheese together with the panko in a small bowl and sprinkle on top of the potatoes. Cover with aluminum foil. Cook for 30 minutes. Remove the cover. If the potatoes are swimming in cream, spoon some off. If they look dry, add a little leftover cream. Cook for 10 to 15 minutes. Remove the potatoes from the oven and preheat the broiler. Broil for 2 to 3 minutes, or until the cheese and panko are browned.

Mashed Potatoes

YIELD: 4–6 SERVINGS

"No Lumps! Every lump is a choking hazard."—Rose Weissman

These potatoes would have been absolutely perfect for Mordecai Glickman. No lumps whatsoever! They do have an obscene amount of fat, though, which is what makes them so incredible.

Comedians are obsessed with removing as much fat from their jokes as possible. We cut out ideas, words, even syllables that don't add to the joke, because those extra bits, those little pieces of fat, blunt the jokes. The opposite is true for mashed potatoes. With mashed potatoes, you want as much fat as they'll take. And they'll take a surprising amount of fat.

I have two rules when I make mashed potatoes: mash as finely as possible, and add more fat.

So, how to mash? Well, you could use a potato masher. Which, if you're going to use a potato masher for anything, mashing potatoes should probably be it. A better tool is the ricer. Better still is the food mill. But the absolute best tool? The key to heavenly, eyes-roll-back-in-your-head mashed potatoes? A tamis. It's a wide, shallow drum with a fine-mesh material on one end. You rest the cooked potatoes on the surface of the mesh and push them through with a spatula or, as I like to use, a silicone bowl scraper.

———

2 pounds (900 g) Yukon Gold potatoes, about 2 inches in diameter
1 stick (113 g) butter, cut into 8 small pieces
2 cups (425 g) heavy cream, warmed in the microwave or in a
    saucepan on the stove (Doesn't need to be hot, just warmed)
2 teaspoons (8 g) kosher salt

Put potatoes in large pot and cover with at least 1 inch of cold water. Turn the heat to high. Once it comes to a gentle simmer, adjust heat to maintain just a gentle simmer. You don't want a full boil, as it could damage the outsides of the potatoes. (If the outsides get damaged, the

potatoes will begin to absorb water, which means they won't absorb as much fat later!) Cook until you can easily pierce the largest potato with a knife. It should slide in smoothly. You shouldn't feel any starchy resistance once they're fully cooked, about 30 minutes. If they're larger, they could take as long as 40 to 50 minutes or longer. Keep that knife handy and, after 20 minutes of simmering, test every 10 minutes.

Drain in a large sieve (or your tamis!) or remove the potatoes from the water with a spider, skimmer, or whatever.

As soon as the potatoes are cool enough to handle, peel them with your fingers.

Meanwhile, put the butter into a large mixing bowl.

Put the potatoes through a ricer, food mill, or my favorite, a tamis. You can process the potatoes directly into the bowl. If you feel more comfortable handling the tamis, you can place a sheet of parchment paper directly on your countertop and process the potatoes through the tamis right onto that sheet.

If you didn't process the potatoes directly into the bowl, add them to the bowl with the butter. Use a wooden spoon and mix to incorporate. Add cream and salt and continue mixing. It will look *very* soupy. Do not worry! Keep stirring and it'll come together. Trust me.

If you don't trust me, add half the cream first, then stir to fully incorporate. Keep adding cream until it won't take any more or you run out.

Maintain at room temp until ready to serve. When ready to serve, reheat in a saucepan over medium-low heat.

Noodle Kugel "Bacon & Eggs"

YIELD: 8 SERVINGS

When I was a kid, I took casseroles for granted. I didn't understand the complex mathematical formula of nutrition, bulk, and ease that a casserole affords to a parent.

You mean, I can combine everything in one pan, throw it in the oven, and when I pull it out, I'll have a happy and full family? Done and DONE!

The downside with casseroles is they tend to lack texture. They fall into that slow-cooker style of texture-less mush.

But they don't have to!

This is one of those dishes where no matter how much extra you THINK you have, you'll find a way to demolish the entire thing faster than your elastic waistband can expand.

If you happen to succeed in saving leftovers, it's perfect for breakfast the next day. I like to perform a magic trick in the morning: I cut a giant square, nuke it for 30 seconds, and surprise everyone with how quickly I eat it.

I get why moms were so into casseroles. They're easy, tasty, and 100 percent healthy. (Don't fact-check that.)

Guanciale is cured pork cheeks (the front ones). If you can't find it, use pancetta. If you can't find pancetta, use bacon. If you can't find bacon, you probably aren't living on Earth, in which case, you should come visit sometime! Bacon's the best thing we've got!

½ pound guanciale, cut into lardons, ¼ inch by ¼ inch by 1 inch
7 tablespoons (100 g) butter
1 tablespoon (10 g) flour
4 cups (1000 g) milk

8 egg yolks
4½ ounces (125 g) Parmigiano-Reggiano cheese, freshly grated
2 teaspoons (6 g grated) nutmeg
1 pound (453 g) penne pasta

Continued on page 118

Preheat oven 350°F.

Add guanciale to a cold skillet large enough to fit it all on one layer. Turn heat to high. Turn heat to low as soon when you hear the sizzle. Cook until one side is browned, then flip each lardon and brown the other side. Once done, transfer guanciale to a paper towel–lined plate.

Make the roux. Melt butter in a small saucepan over medium heat. Add flour to the saucepan, increase heat to medium-high, and stir constantly. You want it hot enough to cook out some of the flour flavor but not so hot that it starts browning. Reduce the heat if it starts browning. Add milk and bring to a simmer while stirring. Simmer for a minute and then remove from heat. Set aside. Let cool for 5 to 10 minutes so it doesn't cook the egg mixture.

Beat egg yolks to combine in a bowl. Add cheese, nutmeg, and roux. Stir to combine. Set aside.

Bring a small pot of salted water (remember, it should taste like the sea) to a rolling boil. Cook the pasta for 4 minutes. Strain and discard the cooking water.

Transfer pasta to a 8 by 8–inch casserole dish.

Add the guanciale and then the custard mix.

Bake 30 to 45 minutes at 350°F.

Pureed Cauliflower with Guanciale and Pesto

YIELD: 2–4 SERVINGS

Cauliflower smells like farts. There's no way around it. Hopefully the Weissmans knew this as Zelda prepared the pureed cauliflower for the failed Mordecai Glickman dinner (spoiler alert: Mordecai's dead). Otherwise they assumed the worst of her. Once you cook it, it smells great. But, if you're like me and like to prep your ingredients ahead of time, know that your fridge may smell like toots until you cook it.

I don't know whether the Weissmans kept kosher all year. For the sake of this recipe, let's assume that they didn't. Rose seeks the advice of a psychic, for goodness sake. If it's difficult for you to picture Rose eating pork, then just imagine this at empty-headed Penny's place.

Bottom line: I don't care who in the Maisel world cooks this—it could be the woman ordering pork in the butcher shop or the doormen for all I care!—as long as someone cooks it. (Can you tell I'm a fan of guanciale?)

4 ounces (100 g) guanciale, cut into lardons ¼-inch by ¼-inch by 1-inch
½ head (600 g) cauliflower, stem removed
½ teaspoon (2 g) kosher salt
½ cup (100 g) pesto (recipe follows)

Add the guanciale to a medium skillet set over high heat. Once the guanciale starts to sizzle, reduce heat to low. Cook until the guanciale is crispy, about 20 minutes. Flip each lardon once about halfway through to crisp the other side. You don't need to stir, toss, or shake the guanciale. Just enjoy your glass of wine.

Continued on page 120

Remove all but 1 tablespoon of the fat from the pan. (You don't need to measure; just estimate.) Tip the pan to pool the fat on one side and spoon it into a jar or metal bowl. You can save it for a flavorful finishing fat. Or discard.

Use a food processor with the grater attachment and grate the cauliflower. Add the cauliflower to the pan and turn the heat up to medium-high. Add kosher salt. Cook for 8 to 10 minutes, until the cauliflower is browned and cooked through. Similar to browning the guanciale, you don't need to stir frequently. The cauliflower is so small that it doesn't take much to cook out the raw flavor. We're focusing our efforts on browning the cauliflower. So, after you add the cauliflower, let it sizzle for a few minutes. Use your nose. If you smell it getting browned and almost burned, stir it. This is a great recipe to develop your cooking intuition because the cauliflower is so forgiving.

Remove from the heat and stir in pesto. The residual heat in the pan will heat the pesto. After mixing, taste it and add more salt as necessary.

Serve as a side to a main dish for 4 people, or on its own for 2 people.

Pesto

Yield: about 2 cups

8 ounces (225 g) basil leaves
8 garlic cloves (40 g)
2 cups (250 g) pine nuts
2 cups (100 g) grated Parmigiano-Reggiano cheese
1¹⁄₃ cups (300 g) olive oil

Process the basil, garlic, and pine nuts into a paste in a food processor. Add the cheese and process to mix. With the processor running, add the olive oil in a slow stream until completely mixed. Transfer to a sealable container and top with a layer of olive oil if not using immediately.

Risotto with Tomatoes, Feta, and Paprika

YIELD: 2 SERVINGS

Risotto isn't difficult to get right. It's impossible.

Cook it too fast, and it's soupy undercooked rice. Too slow? And you'll never get dinner on the table.

What is it about risotto that makes me want to take a nap midway through?

Try as you might to follow a recipe from a famous chef (like me), it never turns out as easy as they claim or as sexy as the pictures look. Oh, you might get close. You might get 90 percent through the recipe, and think to yourself "I've got this!"

You do not got this.

It can be daunting, like doing stand-up right after Lenny Bruce. Here's my suggestion: take the pressure off yourself. Treat each batch of risotto as a learning experience, have a glass of wine, take a Xanax, relax. You'll get through it. And you'll come out a better cook because of it.

32 ounces Chicken Stock (page 90)
4 tablespoons (56 g) butter, divided
2 tablespoons (25 g) olive oil
1 pound (453 g) onions, ½-inch diced
½ cup (100 g) Carnaroli risotto
2 teaspoons (8 g) kosher salt
½ cup (120 g or 120 mL) dry white wine, such as pinot grigio
1 bunch (20 g) thyme, tied with a piece of kitchen twine

1 heaping cup (120 g) cherry tomatoes, halved
2 tablespoons (2 g) thyme
2 teaspoons (6 g) sweet or smoky paprika. Doesn't matter!
½ cup (80 g) feta, crumbled
½ loosely packed cup (3 g) mint

Continued on page 124

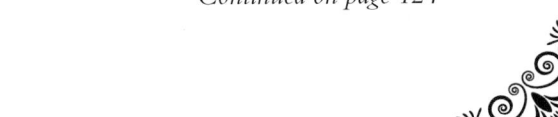

Add chicken stock to a small saucepan, simmer over medium heat.

Add 2 tablespoons butter and olive oil to a large saucepan over medium heat. Add onions to pan and sweat until translucent. Add risotto to the pan and increase heat to medium-high to toast the risotto, stirring continuously to prevent burning. Add the salt and white wine to the pan, stir to incorporate, and cook until the liquid has evaporated.

Add the cherry tomatoes, thyme, and paprika to the pan. Stir to incorporate.

Add ½ cup of chicken stock to the pan, stir constantly, and cook until the liquid has been fully absorbed. Continue adding stock ½ cup at a time and stirring until the liquid has been absorbed.

When the risotto is al dente, remove from the heat and stir in the feta, 2 tablespoons butter, and mint. It's important to stir vigorously at this point. The harder you stir it, the more emulsified the butter and cheese will be. Serve immediately.

Roasted Asparagus with Olive Oil, Pistachio, Parmigiano-Reggiano, and Lemon Zest

YIELD: 2 SERVINGS

Asparagus makes a few appearances on the show. The Maisels have it at the steakhouse when they meet poor, empty-headed Penny for the first (and possibly the last) time. Susie's chowing down on lobster and asparagus at Mary's party while Midge performs a routine with Randall.

They were probably eating steamed asparagus. I could never get behind steamed vegetables. They're so boring! People wonder why they can't get their kids to eat vegetables. Maybe you'd have a chance if you didn't make it taste like grunt! (This dish does not taste like grunt.)

Depending on how hot you want your kitchen to get, you can roast or broil these. I've included both directions below.

---

1 pound (453 g) asparagus
Extra-virgin olive oil, as needed (about 4 – 6 tablespoons)
Kosher salt, to taste (about 1 tablespoon)
¼ cup (30 g) pistachios
¼ cup freshly grated Parmigiano-Reggiano.
Zest of ½ lemon

> **A Note on the Parm:**
> Be warned, store-bought pre-grated Parmigiano-Reggiano generally tastes worse than freshly grated.

Keep the asparagus spears in the bundle they came in. Grab one of them by the thick, woody end (that's what she said) and break it off. Cut the rest at this point so they're all the same length. The point of this exercise is to remove the woody parts at the bottom, and an easy way to find out where the asparagus gets woody is to see where it snaps.

Continued on page 127

Line a baking pan with foil. It makes cleanup so much easier.

Unbundle the asparagus. Set them free! If you're as anal retentive as I am, arrange them in one layer facing the same direction. This also makes plating easier. However you arrange them, make sure they're not stacked. And use a baking pan that's large enough to fit all the asparagus without crowding. These guys need a little space to get hot and brown. Remember, brown is where flavor comes from.

Drizzle with extra-virgin olive oil. Salt to taste. I usually use 4 to 6 tablespoons of oil and 1 tablespoon of kosher salt per pound of asparagus. Remember, most of this stuff will end up on the foil, so you won't be consuming all the oil and salt.

Roasting Method: Preheat the oven to 475°F. Bake for 8 to 10 minutes, or until browned.

Broiling Method: Preheat the broiler to 500°F for at least 10 minutes. Broil for 3 to 5 minutes, or until browned.

The time required will depend on your oven. The goal here is to brown these bad boys without overcooking. You want them firm enough to stand up on their own with a little droop. Too much and they'll have the texture of stringy rubber bands.

Scatter the pistachios, cheese, and lemon zest over the asparagus. Then transfer to a serving plate.

Potato Kugel

The kugel, to me (a gentile), is the epitome of Jewish comfort food. It makes me wish I'd had a bubbe to make this for me. Both the Weissman and Maisel households would have a kugel on rotation. And for good reason. It's easy to prepare, it's so flavorful, and it can feed a large group.

2 pounds (900 g) russet potatoes, grated
¼ cup (35 g) flour
2 tablespoons (25 g) canola oil
1 pound (453 g) onions, ½-inch dice
1 cup (30 g or 1 ounce) green onion, chopped

3 whole eggs
3 egg yolks
2 teaspoons (8 g) kosher salt
½ cup (100 g) crème fraîche
Chives, for garnish

For the potatoes
Fill a large bowl with cold water and set next to your work area. Grate the potatoes using a food processor fitted with the grater attachment or a coarse grater and add to the bowl of water. This will help remove some of the starch, which will help make the kugel lighter. Dry them in a salad spinner or by laying them out on a clean dishcloth. Toss with ¼ cup flour.

For the onions
Heat the oil in a medium skillet over medium heat and add onions. Sweat until translucent, about 10 minutes. Remove to a bowl.

For the custard
Add the 3 whole eggs, the 3 yolks, the salt, and the crème fraîche to a large bowl and mix together.

To complete
Preheat oven to 400°F. Add onions and potatoes to the custard and mix together. Lightly oil a 7 x 9–inch casserole dish with 1 to 2 tablespoons canola oil. Add the potato custard. Bake in a 400°F oven for 45 to 60 minutes or until the top is golden brown and the custard no longer wobbles when you jiggle the dish. Garnish with thinly sliced chives.

Latkes

YIELD: 4–6 LATKES

Baz: "Next time, I'd like some latkes."

Midge: "I make great latkes. Genius latkes. You won't be sorry!"

Oh, Baz. He knows he's in a great position. As long as he gives Joel a terrible time, he can get free brisket. And, while he's got a pink Pyrex full of beautiful brisket, he's got the chutzpah to ask for latkes next time. You gotta hand it to him. He knows what he's doing. At least when it comes to negotiating for food.

You have a few options for cooking this recipe. Instead of creating one giant latke and cutting it after cooking, you could create smaller individual latkes and flip them using a spatula. Or you could use a smaller pan and just make smaller latkes.

They are light and fluffy and crunchy, the holy trinity of potato perfection. Which is a bit confusing in a traditionally Jewish dish.

---

1 pound (453 g) russet potatoes
1 bunch, (4 to 6) green onions
6 tablespoons (80 g) canola oil

Peel and coarsely grate potatoes. If you have a food processor, use the grater attachment to quickly grate all the potatoes. If not, use a box grater and prepare to get a workout.

Immediately put the grated potatoes in a bowl and fill with water. Soak for 10 minutes.

Meanwhile, remove the root and white parts of the green onions and discard. Cut off the darkest green parts—usually the top 3 to 6 inches—of two of the onions and set aside. Make one cut down the length of the green onion tubes, taking care not to split the entire onion into two separate halves. You're just opening up the tube. Then, slice crosswise into ⅛-inch-thick slices.

Continued on page 132

Set aside. We'll use those for a garnish. You can keep the greens in a little tub of water and stick them in the fridge if you're not going to use them for a few hours. It'll keep them nice and crisp.

Slice the rest of the green onions crosswise into ⅛-inch-thick slices. It's okay to mix the light green and dark green parts together for this. Set aside.

Dry the grated potatoes in a salad spinner. If you don't have a salad spinner, drain them in a large sieve, and then dry on a paper towel–lined baking sheet.

Heat ⅛ inch of canola oil in a large nonstick sauté pan over high heat. When it starts to shimmer, reduce heat to medium and carefully add a third of the potatoes. Don't splash the hot oil everywhere. Sprinkle them in like you're a fairy blessing someone with potatoes.

Sprinkle half of the green onions on top of the potatoes. Repeat with another third of the potatoes, and the rest of the green onions. Sprinkle the remaining potatoes on top.

Cook for 5 to 8 minutes, or until well browned.

Use a fish turner or offset spatula to flip the giant latke. Don't hurt yourself.

Cook for another 5 to 8 minutes, or until the other side is browned.

Slide the giant latke onto a paper towel–lined plate. Cut into quarters and serve immediately, topped with the reserved sliced dark green onion. If you reserved them in water, be sure to drain them before using.

The Art of Latke Flipping

There's no high quite like killing it on stage. (I could be wrong . . . I've never done drugs.) But flipping a giant latke comes close.

The hardest part of flipping latke is the mental preparation. It's mandatory that you stress out. It's important that you work yourself into a mental tizzy visualizing the flip. The wrist pop, the midair flip. The oil splattering all over your new Theory shirt or dress. The dog barking in anticipation that, as usual, the latke turning end over end in the air will land on the floor.

But then you stick the landing. The latke falls magically into the pan as if it never left in the first place. The crowd cheers.

You don't have a crowd?

You should totally get yourself a crowd.

Kasha Varnishkes

YIELD: 2 SERVINGS

"Half pastrami on rye, half chopped liver on hallah, stuffed cabbage, some kasha varnishkas, and a bit of arugula. Extremely Jewish and extremely hungry. The pickle's funny."—Herb Smith.

"DOINK."—Herb Smith

"Don't trust a guy who will work for salami."—Susie Myerson

This is not your Bubbe's Kasha Varnishkes. This is my Kasha Varnishkes. This is my take on the classic comfort dish. Same old kasha. Same old varnishkes. With a twist!

I couldn't bring myself to include just another KV recipe in this book. You can search all over the internet for standard KV. You'll find some variation of: kasha, bow-tie pasta, onions, egg, schmaltz. I won't insult you by trying to tweak a regular recipe ever so slightly.

If Herb Smith ordered KV and got this, he'd probably wonder when the owners of the Stage Deli sold to gentiles.

I'm gonna come right out and say it: I don't get kasha. I'm sure it's a favorite for some people. Or they grew up with their Bubbe making it. I tried it the conventional way, and I just couldn't get behind it. It just didn't have enough flavor for me. I'm all for simple dishes, but the traditional kasha varnishkes just didn't make it into the rotation.

So, I changed it a little bit. It still has kasha. It still has varnishkes. It still has schmaltz. But it also has some other stuff.

¼ cup (50 g) kasha

4 tablespoons (50 g) rendered chicken fat or olive oil

¼ pound (40 g before prepping) shallots, ¼-inch dice

½ pound (225 g) mushrooms

½ cup whole milk

¼ cup (75 g) heavy cream

4 tablespoons fresh thyme

2 cups (100 g) bow-tie pasta

Continued on page 135

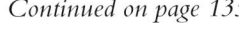

Add the kasha to a sauté pan set over medium heat until toasted. Give them a gentle shake every minute or two to toast evenly. It'll smell nutty. Nutty is good. Transfer the toasted kasha to a small bowl. Set aside.

Add the oil to a large skillet set over medium heat. Add the shallots to the pan. If they start browning, reduce the heat to medium-low.

Add the mushrooms to the pan, toss or stir to combine, and increase the heat to medium-high. Sauté until the mushrooms are browned.

Add the milk, heavy cream, and fresh thyme to the pan, reduce heat to medium, and reduce the liquid by half.

For the pasta
Fill a large saucepan halfway with water. Add salt as needed. The water should taste like the sea. Please salt your pasta water. It'll make this dish taste so much better.

Cook the pasta 1 minute less than the package directions.

To complete
Use a spider to transfer the pasta to the pan with the mushrooms. It's okay if some of the pasta water comes with it. It'll help season the mushrooms.

Add ¼ cup of the pasta water to the pan and simmer for 2 to 3 minutes.

Divide among two plates. Garnish with fresh chives and/or more fresh thyme.

Hangover Mac & Cheese

YIELD: 4 SERVINGS

JOEL: "So, what's going on here?"

MIDGE: "Where?"

JOEL: "The great mac and cheese massacre of 1958."

MIDGE: "I'm hungry."

I've never been hungover (don't fact check that), but I have been hungry. But the first time it happens, I'll make this macaroni and cheese. If it works for Midge, it can work for me.

---

1 cup panko
½ pound (225 g) pasta of your choice
1 pint half-and-half
4 ounces (113 g) Havarti

4 ounces (113 g) Parmigiano-Reggiano
4 ounces (113 g) mascarpone
4 ounces (113 g) white cheddar

Preheat the oven to 350°F.

Toast the panko in a medium skillet over medium heat. Once it's good and toasted, transfer to a small bowl. Set aside.

Cook the pasta for 4 minutes. Drain, and reserve.

Bring the half-and-half to a gentle simmer in a medium saucepan over medium heat. Add the cheeses to the saucepan and stir until completely incorporated. You shouldn't see huge chunks of cheese floating around.

Add the pasta to a 13-by-9-inch baking dish. Pour the cheese on top. Top with panko.

Bake for 30 minutes. If the panko is getting too brown, or the pasta looks like it's drying out, cover the casserole dish with a piece of foil.

Headliners
(Mains)

Braised Chicken Thighs | 141

The Brisket | 142

Fresh Linguine with Ricotta Salata | 146

Papa's Favorite Roast Beef | 147

Schnitzel and Watercress | 149

Rack of Lamb | 151

Midge's Meatloaf | 155

Lamb Curry | 157

Roast Chicken | 160

Sautéed Duck Breast with Watercress Salad | 163

Pan-Seared Roughy with Lemon, Mint, and Chive Butter | 165

Braised Chicken Thighs

YIELD: 4–6 SERVINGS

Zelda deserves a few nights off, for all she does for the Weissmans.

---

4 chicken thigh and leg quarters (4 thighs
　and 4 legs)
Kosher salt, as needed
4 tablespoons (50 g) canola oil
8 cloves garlic (6 g)
1 pound (453 g) potatoes, ½-inch dice
2 onions, cut into wedges

½ pound (225 g) shallots
1 lemon, ⅛-inch slices, plus 1 lemon, halved,
　for lemon juice garnish
4 tablespoons (30 g) capers
4 tablespoons (30 g) green olives, diced
4 tablespoons (10 g) dill
4 tablespoons (10 g) parsley, for garnish

Preheat the oven to 350°F.

Pat the chicken dry with paper towels. Season with kosher salt.

Add oil to a heavy-bottomed Dutch oven and heat over medium heat. Add chicken skin-side down and cook for 8 minutes. Remove the chicken to a cooling rack on a foil-lined baking sheet.

Smoosh (technical term) garlic under the broad side of a chef's knife. Leave the skin on and add to the pan. Cook until the garlic is lightly browned, tilting the pan to cook the garlic in pooled oil. Once the garlic is browned, remove and discard.

Add the potatoes, onions, shallots, and lemon wheels to the pan. Place chicken on top of the vegetables and move the pan to the oven. Cook, uncovered, for 45 minutes, or until chicken is cooked through. You can use an instant-read thermometer to test for doneness (155°F). Chicken legs are pretty forgiving to overcooking, so I tend to just go by time.

To complete, divide the potatoes and onions among 4 plates and place the chicken on top. Top with capers, olives, dill, a squeeze of lemon, and parsley.

The Brisket

YIELD: *6–8 SERVINGS*

You've gotta love Midge's unwavering support of Joel's comedy career, especially her knack for getting Joel better time slots. Stand-up can be a grind. In the current New York comedy scene, fledgling comedians perform on "bringer shows"—comedians bring paying audience members in exchange for a spot on the show. I perform at a club with a ten-person bringer requirement. When I first started out, I didn't have ten friends (I still don't) so I did favors (wink) for the producer.

Even if you don't do stand-up, the Brisket can grease the wheels on any important thing you need done. Need your car fixed? Brisket. Want a promotion? Brisket. Need your neighbor to do some weird favor involving a snow shovel, some rope, and a petting zoo? Brisket.

This brisket is easy enough to be a weeknight meal but would be equally at home for a special occasion.

---

1 pound (453 g) carrots, ½-inch dice
1 pound (453 g) celery, ½-inch dice
1 pound (453 g) onions, ½-inch dice
1 brisket, 3–5 pounds, fat and silverskin
    trimmed (I prefer only a thin strip of fat
    on top)

Kosher salt, as needed
4 tablespoons (50 g) canola oil
1 750 ml bottle of dry red wine, such as
    cabernet sauvignon or merlot
32 ounces (1 L) beef stock
Maldon sea salt, as needed

Preheat the oven to 275°F.

For the vegetables
Wash the carrots by running them under cold water and rubbing them with your fingers. The point here is to dislodge any dirt. We're not going to be eating the carrots in the end, so presentation isn't as important. Dry the carrots with a dish towel. Remove the root end and cut lengthwise to halve each carrot. Cut lengthwise again to quarter the carrots. Cut crosswise into 4-inch-long sticks. Congrats, you've just made carrot sticks! We want ¼-inch-thick dice for this preparation,

so cut each stick crosswise into ¼-inch-thick slices. You can group three or four sticks together to speed up this process. Set aside in a small bowl.

Remove the root end of the celery by cutting crosswise about 1 to 2 inches up from the root. You want to remove the root and the whitest parts of the celery. Separate the stalks and wash, using your fingers to dislodge any dirt. Dry, cut into 4-inch-long sticks, then cut crosswise into ½-inch-thick slices. Set aside in a small bowl.

Remove the top (opposite the root end) of each onion. Stand the onion on the cut side and cut in half through the root end. Remove the dry outer layers. With the large cut side down, slice downward every ¼ inch, making sure not to cut all the way through the onion. Hold the onion from the top and make horizontal cuts every ¼ inch. Now, make vertical cuts every ¼ inch down the length of the onion. You've just diced an onion! Set aside.

Continued on page 145

For the brisket

Trim excess fat and silverskin. Salt the entire exterior of the brisket. Grab a few fingers' worth of kosher salt and sprinkle over the meat from a height of at least 12 inches. Why so high? Because this results in a more even coating of salt. Don't worry about the amount of salt you're using here. This may seem like a lot, but remember, that there's a *lot* of meat beneath the surface, and a lot of the salt falls off in the cooking process. Repeat for all sides of the brisket.

Heat 3 tablespoons of canola oil in a large pan over high heat. When the oil begins to shimmer, carefully add the brisket—try to avoid splattering everywhere, cussing, and having your spouse roll her eyes at you while suggesting you just order pizza and try to be a man. When the meat is browned on its first side, after about 2 to 4 minutes, flip it to another side. Repeat until all sides are browned, about 12 minutes total. If a side sticks, give it another minute instead of forcing it up. Once complete, remove the brisket from the pan and set aside. Spoon the fat out of the pan. It's served its purpose, and will only dilute the flavor in the completed dish. Do not wipe the pan clean.

The pan should have brown stuff stuck to the bottom. This is good. This is flavor. We're going to deglaze the pan, freeing up that yummy brown stuff. The brown stuff is technically called fond. And I'm fond of fond.

Turn the heat to medium, add the wine, and use a wooden spatula to scrape up the brown bits. This is called *deglazing*. Reduce the wine to a glaze, about 15 minutes. Remove from heat.

Add the brisket back to the pan. Optionally, and to make things easier in the final steps, cut a piece of cheesecloth larger than the pan and cover the meat. Add the onions, carrots, and celery on top of the cheesecloth. Add enough beef stock to cover everything. Gather the cheesecloth and place it inside the pan. Place the pan over high heat and bring the liquid to a simmer. Remember, simmer does not mean a boil. You should see water vapor coming off the top, but it shouldn't be bubbling. Once it reaches a simmer, cover and place in the oven. Cook for 5 hours, or until the meat is fork tender. If you're in a rush, you can increase the heat to 325°F and cook for less time, but the meat won't be as tender.

To complete

Remove the pan from the oven. Gather the edges of the cheesecloth, lift the vegetables out of the pan and reserve to a large bowl. Remove the brisket to a cooling rack to drain for a moment, and then transfer to a cutting board.

Heat the remaining liquid in the Dutch oven over medium high heat and reduce by half to concentrate the flavors. Reserve.

Slice the brisket across the grain into ¼-inch-thick slices. Don't know where the grain is? Grab a corner of the brisket and pull. You should end up with a long strand of meat. That is the direction of the grain. Cut across that. Arrange the slices on a serving platter. Scatter the reserved vegetables around the meat and drizzle some of the reserved sauce over the whole thing. Top with a few generous pinches of Maldon sea salt.

Fresh Linguine with Ricotta Salata

Yield: 4 servings

I added this dish especially for Midge. She's juggling a lot of balls. With her day job at B. Altman and her night job on stage, she's short on time to take care of Ethan and her daughter (although with as little we see her daughter, I'm guessing she doesn't eat much?). Midge seems busy, and this dish is perfect for busy people. It takes 15 minutes to throw together, and that includes the time it takes to boil water.

It's important to salt the pasta water correctly since we'll be using it in the final dish. Not only will it season the pasta, but it's also going to season the sauce. So don't mess it up.

The key to not messing up this recipe is tasting the pasta water before adding pasta. It should taste like the ocean. (Hint: salty.) It should be noticeably salty, but not so much that it burns. If you add too much salt, carefully remove some of the salted water and replace with fresh water. If you add too little . . . just add more!

1 pound (453 g) fresh linguine
1½ cups (60 g) ricotta salata, grated
Kosher salt, to taste (see headnote above)

Cook pasta 1 minute less than the directions state.

Using a measuring cup, transfer 1 cup of the pasta water to a pan heating over medium. Add the cheese to the water in the pan, stir to combine.

Use tongs to move the pasta to the pan. Stir to combine and cook until most of the water has been absorbed or evaporated. If you want it a little saucier, add more pasta water.

Papa's Favorite Roast Beef

YIELD: 8–10 SERVINGS

Papa deserves this. After everything he's been through. Having his son-in-law move out on his daughter. Not being able to read after dinner because Ethan is too busy plugged into the boob tube. Having to live in a fort made of his own books.

This is great for a dinner party. It looks so fancy. And it's so easy. Pair this with the Hangover Mac & Cheese (page 137), maybe some Roasted Asparagus (page 125) or Blistered Green Beans (page 109) for some veggies, and you will be a hit at your next dinner party.

This will work for any size rib roast. One common suggestion is 1 rib for 2 to 3 people so a 4-rib roast will serve 8 to 10 people. You can scale this up or down depending on the servings required. The cooking time will be roughly the same.

2 egg whites
1 (4-rib) standing rib roast
Kosher salt, as needed

Cracked pepper, as needed
3 tablespoons (20 g) black peppercorns
1 cup (40 g) rosemary and/or thyme

Ask the butcher for a four-rib standing rib roast. Ask him or her to French it, which will make your presentation super sexy. Have them remove the bones but then reattach them with twine. That'll make it easier to serve.

Whisk the egg whites and brush on the rib roast. You may not need all the whites. Season the meat on all sides with salt and pepper. Put the herbs on a piece of parchment paper. Roll the roast in the herbs.

Put the roast on a cooling rack set in a foil-lined baking sheet. You can use a roasting pan or a large skillet. Insert the probe thermometer through one of the small sides, as close to the center of the meat as possible.

Preheat the oven to 225°F and roast the . . . roast . . . until the thermometer reads 130–133°F, about 2 hours. Pull it out to rest for 25 minutes. About 15 minutes before serving, heat the oven to 500°F and roast it at 500°F for 8 to 10 minutes. This will help develop the herb crust and, personally, I like when my roast feels like it came right from the oven.

Schnitzel and Watercress

YIELD: 2–4 SERVINGS

We don't see anyone eat schnitzel in the first season of *The Marvelous Mrs. Maisel*, but I'd imagine Rose would include this in the rotation when they're craving comfort food. I'm sure Zelda wouldn't mind how easy it is to prepare, either.

Schnitzel is often pounded to a thickness of ⅛ inch. But, depending on your mood, and your level of laziness, you can get away with buying thin cut chicken breasts, which run about ½ inch thick. For ½ inch thick, cook for 3 minutes on one side (the presentation side), and 2 minutes on the next. For ⅛ inch thick, cook 3 to 4 minutes total.

I like watercress most when it's undressed. (Don't make it weird.) If you're feeling gregarious, you can toss it with a tablespoon or two of olive or canola oil, a squeeze of lemon, and a pinch of kosher salt.

4 (4-ounce) skinless, boneless chicken breasts, pounded to ⅛-inch thickness or not!
⅓ cup (50 g) flour
1 egg (55 g)
¾ cup (75 g) panko
Canola oil, as needed
2 teaspoons (5 g) chili powder, optional
Kosher salt, to taste
Smoked sea salt, as needed (if you can't find smoked sea salt, use regular sea salt)
Lemon wedges for garnish

For the salad:
3 tablespoons olive or canola oil
1 tablespoon lemon juice
Salt, to taste
1 bunch watercress

Continued on page 150

This is a great dish to practice your mise en place. Arrange three bowls on your work surface. Add the flour to the first, the egg to the second, and the panko to the third.

Prepare another plate to hold the dredged chicken.

Get a skillet—or, if you want to contain more of the splattering oil because you're super lazy like me, a large Dutch oven—all set up. And by all set up, I just mean put it on the stove.

Don't forget to line a plate with paper towels and set it near the stove to hold the finished schnitzels.

Finally, like an assembly line, dredge the chicken through the flour, then egg, then panko, then the holding plate.

Add oil to the skillet or Dutch oven and warm over medium heat. Once the oil is shimmering, add the chicken. Work in batches. You don't want to crowd them. If you pounded them to ⅛-inch thick, cook for 2 minutes on each side. If the chicken breasts are ½-inch thick, cook for 3 minutes on one side and 2 minutes on the next.

After cooking, move them to the paper towel–lined plate and sprinkle with a generous pinch of sea salt. I like to include a few lemon wedges on the plates so folks can decide for themselves how much lemon to add.

For the salad
Whisk together the oil, lemon, and salt to taste in the base of a large bowl. Add the watercress and toss to dress.

Rack of Lamb

YIELD: 2–4 SERVINGS

"Rabbi loves his lamb!"

All right, you scored the rabbi for Yom Kippur! Congratulations. Next on the to-do list: what to cook? Well, if your rabbi is anything like Midge's, you're going to want to serve lamb, because "Rabbi loves his lamb!" (Duh.)

But, what happens if your spouse just left you—for a shorthand girl, even!—and you're left to cook the whole thing yourself? You need a no-brainer recipe. Something you can throw together without too much fuss. Something that'll free you up to cook the rest of the meal.

Enter . . . the Rack of Lamb.

Oh. My. God. I'd forgotten how easy it was to cook a rack of lamb.

Lamb makes several appearances in *The Marvelous Mrs. Maisel*. It's an impressive dish to cook for a boss/lover/yourself.

Tips: Ask the butcher to French it for you. (Don't worry, it's not as gross as it sounds.) Frenching it just means they remove some of the meat between the bones and clean up the ends of the ribs for presentation purposes. Frenching is a much cleaner, more impressive, presentation.

Regardless of who Frenches your bones (hehe), make sure to save the trimmings. You can use them for stock or stew.

This is almost set-it-and-forget-it easy. You can set it, just don't forget it. This lamb is so good you might want to consider doubling this recipe.

1 rack of lamb
1 cup packed (40 g) mint leaves
3 – 4 garlic cloves

⅓ cup olive oil
Kosher salt

Continued on page 153

Set a large skillet over medium-high heat. Add rack of lamb, fat-cap side down, and sear for 4 minutes. Use a clean dishtowel or a few paper towels to press down on the rack to ensure contact between the fat cap and the skillet.

Transfer to a roasting pan, or a cooling rack on a foil-lined baking sheet, and rest the meat for 30 minutes.

Preheat the oven to 170°F, or as low as your oven will go.

Insert a probe thermometer into the side of the rack, into the thickest part of the meat. Cook until the core temperature hits 136°F for medium rare, 144°F for medium, about 2 hours.

Combine the mint, garlic, olive oil, and kosher salt in a food processor and process until it forms a paste. Reserve.

When lamb is done, top with the paste and serve.

A Note About Lamb

People often complain about lamb's gaminess. Make no mistake, gaminess does not equal lambiness. The wonks in other more science-y cookbooks (like *Modernist Cuisine*, where I originally learned about this slow/low cooking method) explain that gaminess comes from oxidized fat. Basically, if your lamb isn't properly cared for after it's not living anymore, it runs the risk of gaminess.

What can you do to prevent that?

Buy from a reputable butcher. Ask him/her how fresh it is. I've seen a lot more vacuum-packed lamb recently and I've never had a problem with it. The less airtime lamb has, the better it'll be. Be sure to remove as much excess fat and silverskin (the shiny stuff that encloses muscle tissue) as you can before cooking. You should be doing this anyway, as that stuff is unappetizing in a finished dish.

Midge's Meatloaf

YIELD: 2–4 SERVINGS

MIDGE: "So . . . you stole Bob Newhart's act."

JOEL: "It's fine. Everybody does it. It's no big deal."

MIDGE: "It's not? Because when I found out June Friedman used my meatloaf recipe, I almost stabbed her in the eye with a fork."

For the record, I did not steal this recipe from Midge. It's on extended loan. That she doesn't know about. Also, June Friedman is a total skank.

Stealing is a no-no in comedy. If you're not strong enough to come up with your own material, you're not going anywhere in comedy.

Some comics do nothing but street jokes—jokes that everyone knows, that anyone can Google—and wonder why their careers aren't going anywhere. It's because their jokes aren't original. They don't have their own acts.

The idea that Joel wants to be a comedian so bad that he steals Bob Newhart's act is tragic. He tries. He's struggling with his comedy, with keeping his hands off that empty-headed Penny Pan. But he's trying.

Unfortunately, by copying another comic's act, he's not staying true as an artist, as a comic, and as a man. OR as a husband.

In comedy, jokes are like recipes. Which raises the question: why am I giving you all my recipes? I guess publishing my recipes is like publishing a comedy special: once it's out in the world, I'll stop telling those jokes. They're no longer my jokes. They're your jokes. They're no longer my recipes, they're OUR recipes. (They're still my recipes and I'll stab you in the eye with a fork if you steal them.)

Continued on page 156

2 tablespoons (30 g) butter
2 cups (225 g) onions, ¼-inch dice
¼ cup dry white wine
1 tablespoon Better Than Bouillon
1 cup (100 g) stale bread, broken into bite-sized chunks
½ cup (125 g) whole milk
1 pound (453 g) ground turkey
1 pound (453 g) ground beef
2 extra large eggs
2 teaspoons (8 g) kosher salt
4 ounces (113 g) cheese
½ cup panko

Add the butter and onions to a large sauté pan and sweat over medium-low heat until the onions caramelize, about 60 minutes, stirring occasionally. If the onions get too dry, add a few tablespoons of water and stir. You're not trying to brown the onions, you're trying to caramelize them. If they start browning, turn the heat to low. You should hear a gentle sizzling, but nothing more.

Add the wine and the Better Than Bouillon to the onions. Use a wood spatula to scrape up any brown bits stuck to the pan. Cook over medium heat until the wine is almost entirely evaporated. Set aside.

Mix the bread and milk together in a small bowl and let sit for 5 minutes. Discard any unabsorbed milk and squeeze the bread to wring out some of the milk. Move the bread to a large bowl.

Add the ground turkey, ground beef, the eggs, and the salt to the large bowl and mix to combine. Be gentle. The harder you work the meat now, the denser the meatloaf's texture will be later.

Turn out the mixture onto a large piece of parchment paper and shape the meat mixture into a rectangle roughly 7 inches wide by 9 inches long by ½ inch tall. Don't stress over the numbers. This doesn't need to be exact.

Sprinkle the cheese over the meat mixture. Rotate the parchment paper so that one of the shorter sides is closest to you. Working from the bottom, roll the meat into a log shape, peeling back the parchment paper as you roll so the paper isn't included inside the roll.

Scatter the panko over another piece of parchment paper. Roll the loaf in the panko to coat. Transfer the loaf to a foil-lined baking sheet and roast for 45 minutes at 375°F.

Lamb Curry

YIELD: 2–4 SERVINGS

"We can take the lamb curry off the children-approved meals. Zelda gave Ethan a peanut butter sandwich and sent him to bed."—Rose Weissman

I hope you're not as picky as Ethan, because then you'd miss out on this wonderful dish.

I don't know whether this recipe is easier with or without a food processor. On the one hand, it speeds up cutting the onions and ginger. On the other, you have to clean the food processor. Your call!

I like the smoother consistency that pureeing the ingredients gives. Also—and promise me you won't tell all your professional chef friends—but you can skip the browning the meat if you really want to. I live in a tiny apartment, and there are some nights I'd rather not set off the smoke alarm.

I like serving this just like the Weissmans did, with white rice, pita, a simple salad, and wine (my favorite part). Though the Weissmans are drinking red, I prefer a glass of sparkling rosé such as the Italian Franciacorta, a Grüner Veltliner, or an Alsatian Riesling.

My wife thinks I'm crazy, but whenever we order Indian food, I love having cold leftovers the next morning. So I tried the same with this. And it was fantastic. If you're anything like me (insane), you don't normally like stewed dishes in the summer. But give this a shot; I think you'll enjoy it.

---

1 pound (453 g) onions
2 tablespoons fresh ginger
6 cloves (30 g) garlic
1 pound (453 g) boneless lamb
¼ cup (55 g) cream
2 teaspoons (5 g) ground turmeric
2 teaspoons (5 g) cumin
14 ounces (400 g) canned tomatoes

16 ounces (500 g) lamb stock If you don't have lamb stock, you can substitute Chicken Stock (page 90)
Kosher salt, as needed
Oil, as needed
1 cinnamon stick
Flat-leaf parsley, roughly chopped (optional garnish)
Crème fraîche (optional garnish)

Continued on page 159

Food processor method

Remove the skin and root ends of the onions and cut into large chunks. Peel the ginger and cut into small chunks. Use a large chef's knife to lightly crush the garlic cloves. Peel them and discard the skins. Rough chop the onions, ginger, and garlic, add to the food processor. and process until pureed. Reserve.

Non–food processor method

Cut the onions in ¼ inch dice. Peel the ginger and grate it with a fine grater. Lightly smoosh (technical term) the garlic under the broad side of your chef's knife to loosen the peel. Remove the peel, and mince the garlic. Reserve.

Brown the lamb. Use paper towels to pat dry the lamb. Then cut the lamb into 1-inch cubes. Sprinkle plenty of kosher salt over the lamb. Heat a large enameled Dutch oven over medium-high heat. Add enough oil to cover the bottom the pan with about ⅛-inch deep. Working in batches, add the lamb and brown on all sides, about 2 minutes per side. Don't add it all at once unless they all fit in one layer. If you add it all at once, you run the risk of cooling the pan so much that the meat takes longer to brown. The longer it takes to brown, the more you risk overcooking the lamb. Use tongs to turn the lamb. If they stick to the pan, give them another minute or two. Remove the lamb and reserve.

Remove the pan from the heat and use a spoon to remove the oil from the pan. This stuff is spent, and we don't want it messing up the flavor of our curry.

Sweat vegetables. Add the pureed or diced onions/ginger/garlic mixture and sweat over medium-low heat. We're not looking to brown the onions and garlic. We want to cook or "sweat" them until they turn translucent, about 10 minutes.

Preheat the oven to 300°F.

Add cream, turmeric, cumin, tomatoes, stock, cinnamon stick, and lamb to the Dutch oven containing the sweated onion mixture. Bring to a simmer over medium heat and transfer to the oven. Braise in oven until fork-tender, about 2 hours.

Serve with basmati rice and warmed pita like the Weissmans or as cold leftovers like I do. Either way, garnish with parsley and/or a dollop of crème fraîche.

Roast Chicken

This is a no-fuss, no-muss, no-truss roast chicken recipe. It does not get any easier than this, folks. The focus here is the chicken, since it's pretty much the only ingredient.

1 chicken
Kosher salt, as needed

Dry the bird inside and out with paper towels. Moisture will prevent the skin from developing that characteristic crisp. Remove as much of it as possible.

Rain kosher salt upon it. All over it. Top. Bottom. Inside the cavity.

If it has its wingtips, bend those behind the back of the bird. This will help protect the breast meat from drying out.

Preheat the oven to 450°F.

Line a baking sheet with foil and place a cooling rack on the sheet. Put the chicken on the cooling rack and put it on an oven rack in the middle of the oven, legs first and the head (or where the head would be) near the door. The door is the coolest part of the oven. We put the breasts there because we don't want those puppies drying out.

Cook for 45 to 60 minutes.

Remove the chicken from the oven and rest for 10 to 15 minutes. The rest is important! While it cools, the muscle tissue will reabsorb some of the juices, which will make for a moister meat. While we're talking about juices, the whole "cook until the juices run clear" thing is bunk. If you're concerned about undercooking, test it with an instant-read thermometer. You want it to read 155°F. Also, while it's resting, don't tent it. That will just steam it, causing the skin to lose the crispiness we worked so hard for.

I prefer to break the bird down and plate it in the kitchen, so I can avoid the embarrassment of not knowing how to carve a chicken tableside. Keep your phone handy so you can google "how to carve a chicken."

Sautéed Duck Breast with Watercress Salad

YIELD: 2–4 SERVINGS

If pork is the other white meat, duck is the other red meat. And it has something red meat can never touch: crispy skin.

It has the crispy skin of chicken and meatiness of red meat. It's the Frankenstein of the meat world! Some may cry fowl at my reference (and my poultry puns), but I didn't want to write the word "monster," as in "Frankenstein's monster," in a cookbook. (Now look what you made me do.)

A note on the serving size: Duck breasts are around eight ounces apiece, which makes them large enough to split for a lighter meal, as my wife and I often do. If I'm still hungry (or even if I'm not), I'll have some extra Crème Fraîche Cheesecake (page 185) or Chocolate Almond Cake (page 178).

2 duck breasts, roughly 8 ounces each
Kosher salt, as needed
1 tablespoon (10 g) olive oil
1 teaspoon (20 g) lemon juice
3 cups (100 g) watercress

Score the fat on the duck breast. Use a sharp knife and slice the fat every ½ inch. Be careful not to cut into the flesh. We're just scoring the fat so it renders better. Salt both sides of the duck.

Set a medium skillet over medium heat. Lay the duck breasts in the pan skin-side down and lower the heat to medium-low. Tilt the pan and spoon the fat out as it renders. I recommend saving this fat. I use it for sautéing spinach for breakfast. It's delightfully flavorful.

Continued on page 164

Cook for 16 to 18 minutes. If the skin browns too quickly, reduce the heat to low. Flip the breasts over and cook for 1 to 2 minutes more.

If you prefer the precision of a thermometer—and there is no shame in that!—insert a probe thermometer and stop cooking when it reaches 135°F (58°F). Make sure to insert through the end of the breast to ensure you take the temperature of the center of the meat, not the edge.

For the salad
Whisk together oil, vinegar, and salt in the base of a large bowl. Cut the watercress into 2- to 3-inch-long pieces and add to the bowl. Toss to combine. There is not much dressing here, and that's on purpose. I like watercress with little to no dressing, but feel free to add more if you wish.

To complete
Slice the duck breast into ¾-inch-wide pieces. You could go across the breast, as I've done in this photo, or you could go lengthwise for a more dramatic preparation. Serve with dressed watercress.

Pan-Seared Roughy with Lemon, Mint, and Chive Butter

YIELD: 2 SERVINGS

We don't see much fish in the *Marvelous Mrs. Maisel* world. Which is a shame. Fish are funny. Especially the clown fish! (Though they're too slapstick for me . . .) Astrid is surprised her gefilte fish gift goes missing, and Susie's happy as a clam (which she ate, by the way) to get her claws on some lobster. I hope she figured out the best way to hide it under her hat.

This is a great recipe to keep in your tackle box of recipes. It's quick and easy enough for a school night, but light and elegant enough for a date night. (I never want heavy foods for date night.) Throw some Blistered Green Beans (page 109) or Roasted Asparagus (page 125) on the plate for an easy side.

If you can't find orange roughy, you're not exactly off the hook. I'd recommend staying away from swordfish and other meatier fishes for this preparation, but you can use whatever type of fish looks freshest. Ask your fishmonger. Use your nose.

Speaking of which . . . The seafood counter should smell like seafood, which means it should not smell *at all*. My rule: if it smells like fish, cut bait and run.

---

2 (8-ounces, 225 g total) fish fillets
Kosher salt
4 tablespoons (56 g) butter
½ cup (20 g) green onions, ¼-inch slice
4 tablespoons (4 g) mint
2 tablespoons (2 g) chive
4 tablespoons (30 g) nonpareil capers
2 tablespoons fresh squeezed lemon juice

Continued on page 167

Pat the fish dry with paper towels and sprinkle with kosher salt.

Add the butter to a medium nonstick skillet over medium heat. When the butter starts to bubble, add the fish.

Sprinkle the green onions over the fish and, tilting the pan, use a spoon to baste the fish for 5 minutes. Use a fish turner to turn the fish.

Add the mint, chives, and capers to the pan and continue basting for 2 minutes. Use the fish turner to move the fish to a paper towel–lined plate.

Divide the fish between two plates and top with the mint, chive, and butter from the pan.

Drizzle the fresh-squeezed lemon juice over the fish.

For an optional, fancy-looking garnish, use green onion strips. To do so, slice down the length of the green onion, then slice on a severe bias.

Encore!
Desserts

Almond Flan | 170

Black & White Cookie | 173

Brown Butter Rugelach | 175

Chocolate Almond Cake | 178

Chocolate Pudding | 182

Crème Fraîche Cheesecake | 185

Parisian Cocoa | 188

Peanut Butter Cookies | 191

Zagnut | 192

Almond Flan

YIELD: 2–4 SERVINGS

1¼ cups (300 g) milk
1 teaspoon (4 g) kosher salt
¼ cup (50 g) sugar
3 eggs
1 egg yolk
¼ teaspoon vanilla extract
¼ teaspoon almond extract

Preheat the oven to 350°F.

In a small saucepan, warm the milk, salt, and sugar over medium heat until the sugar dissolves. Remove from the heat and let cool for 10 minutes.

In a large bowl, beat the eggs, egg yolk, and vanilla and almond extracts. Add ⅓ of the warm milk to the eggs and stir to combine. Add the remaining milk and stir.

Divide the custard between two 8-ounce ramekins. Place the ramekins into a larger baking sheet, fill with hot water about ⅔ the way up the sides of the ramekins. Wrap plastic wrap around the whole baking sheet. Put into the oven and bake until only the center of each custard wobbles when jostled, about 45 minutes.

Black & White Cookie

YIELD: *ABOUT 12* COOKIES

The doorman has a special place in the hearts of New Yorkers. They're part guardian angel, part sentinel. They hail a cab for you when it's pouring and there's only one available cab for 12 billion New Yorkers, and they protect you from the riffraff (anyone else) outside your building. If you look close enough, under their uniforms, they're wearing capes. It's customary to tip your doormen every Christmas—a small price to pay for the favors (miracles) they perform.

Which is why it's no surprise that Midge buys her doormen black and white cookies.

Black and white cookies are perfect for people who can't make up their minds.

Me: *"I want a cookie!"*

Cookie man: *"Chocolate or vanilla?"*

Me: *"Yes!"*

The most difficult thing about eating a black and white cookie is deciding which color goes in my mouth first. Sometimes it's black. Sometimes it's white. Sometimes, if I'm being honest, I'll fold the cookie in half so I get both at the same time.

These are less cakey than the traditional black and white, and they feature a nice little twist: brown butter. That's right! Black, white, *and* brown… All shades are welcome. (It's an equal-opportunity cookie.)

---

8 ounces (226 g) butter, divided
3/4 cup (150 g) sugar
1 egg
1 teaspoon (4 3/4 g) vanilla extract
1 teaspoon (5 1/3 g) almond extract
1 teaspoon (5 g) baking powder

Continued on page 174

1 teaspoon (4 g) salt
1½ cups (225 g) flour

Vanilla Frosting:
1 cup (100 g) powdered sugar
1 tablespoon (15 g) water

Chocolate Frosting:
4 ounces (125 g) semisweet chocolate
3 tablespoons (40 g) butter

Add half the butter to a small sauté pan and brown it over medium heat. The butter will melt, then bubble, then bubble even smaller. Once the bubbles get very small, froth-like, watch closely. It'll begin to brown. The goal is to get as brown as possible without burning it. If you feel like it's getting close to burning, remove from heat and pour into a heatproof bowl. Set aside to cool for 20 minutes.

Use a hand mixer to cream together the sugar, the reserved brown butter, the egg, and the remaining butter. Add the vanilla and almond extracts and mix together.

In a separate bowl, mix the flour, baking powder, and salt. Add to the creamed butter and mix.

Preheat the oven to 325°F.

Spoon flatware teaspoon-sized balls of batter on a parchment paper-lined baking sheet, with 2 inches of space between the balls. Bake for 15 minutes, or until the cookies are golden brown. Remove from the oven and let cool to room temperature.

For the chocolate frosting
Add the semisweet chocolate and butter to a microwave safe bowl, cover with plastic wrap, and microwave for 2 minutes on 30 percent. Stir to mix. Set aside.

For vanilla frosting
Whisk together the confectioners' sugar, water, and vanilla extract in a small bowl.

To complete
Use a spoon, offset spatula, or butter knife to frost the cookies with half white and half black frosting.

Brown Butter Rugelach

YIELD: *16* COOKIES

How much do I love Herb Smith? Exactly as much as Vern, with every bone in my body.

He's is one of my favorite cameos. Such confidence, such charisma, and such poor joke-writing skills. Did anyone else want him to tell Midge "never wage a land war in Asia" and "never go against a Sicilian when death is on the line"? I kept waiting for him to laugh hysterically and tip over. That never arrived. But his pickle did! (The pickle's funny.)

I loved his giant order at the Stage Deli. "A half pastrami on rye, and a half-chopped liver on challah, a stuffed cabbage, some kasha varnishkes, and a bit of arugula." The first time I watched, I thought his order contained "a bit of *rugelach*." When I rewatched it with the captions—after I decided to include this rugelach recipe, and after I wrote, tested, and photographed it—I found out he actually ordered *arugula*.

So.

Here's a bit of rugelach for you. I'm sure Herb would've appreciated the surprise with his order if the waitress had misheard, too.

———

4 ounces (114 g) butter, divided
4 ounces (114 g) cream cheese
1 cup (150 g) flour
¼ teaspoon (1 g) kosher salt
½ cup (100 g) jam of your choice (I love blackberry, raspberry,
    or a combination of the two.)
1 egg (55 g)
Maldon sea salt, as needed
Turbinado sugar, as needed

Continued on page 177

Add half the butter to a large mixing bowl. Set aside.

Add the remaining butter to a small skillet over medium heat. You don't need to stir. It will melt, then bubble, then brown. Watch it closely once it starts smelling nutty. It doesn't take much time to go from brown to burned. Pour it into the bowl containing the rest of the butter. Use a silicone spatula to scrape all the little brown bits into the bowl.

Add the cream cheese to the bowl and stir to mix the ingredients together. You only need to mix enough so that you don't splatter the liquid everywhere in the next step. (I found this out the hard way . . .)

Use an electric hand mixer to cream the butter and cream cheese in a large bowl.

Add the flour and salt and mix on low until incorporated.

Turn out the dough onto a piece of parchment paper and compress it into a ball. Wrap with plastic wrap and refrigerate for at least 2 hours or up to 24 hours.

Line a large baking sheet (or two smaller baking sheets) with parchment paper. Set aside.

Divide the dough in half. Place one half, flat-side down, onto a piece of parchment paper. Cover with another piece of parchment paper and roll into a disc about 9 inches wide. It's okay if the sides crack while you're rolling. Depending on how much of a perfectionist you are, you can pull off the cracked parts and press them into other parts of the dough to make it more disc like.

Spoon half the jam onto the disc. Use a paring knife to slice the discs into 8 equal wedges. Roll each wedge in on itself, starting with the wide end and working inward, and place on the parchment paper–lined baking sheet.

Refrigerate for at least 20 minutes.

Preheat the oven to 375°F.

Beat the egg in a small bowl. Use a small brush to paint each rugelach with egg. Sprinkle with Maldon sea salt and coarse sugar.

Bake for 15 to 20 minutes, or until the rugelach are golden brown.

Chocolate Almond Cake

I can't recommend Vahlrona cocoa powder highly enough. It's worlds better than the others. It's like the Lenny Bruce of cocoa powder. Except it's never been to jail.

———··•··———

7 ounces (200 g) Almond Paste (page 181)
¼ cup (60 g) sugar
4 ounces (113 g) butter, plus extra to grease the pan
2 tablespoon (40 g) honey
3 eggs
2 tablespoons (30 g) amaretto liqueur, such as Luxardo
⅓ cup (50 g) flour
¼ cup (30 g) cocoa powder
Kosher salt, to taste
1 handful chocolate chips
½ cup sliced almonds
Confectioners' sugar

Mix together the almond paste and the sugar in a large bowl. Add the butter and use a hand mixer to cream the mixture. This is an important step! Creaming things results in a lighter, less dense texture.

Add the honey to the batter and mix to incorporate.

Add the eggs, one at a time, mixing fully to incorporate before adding the next egg.

Add the amaretto, the flour, the cocoa powder, and the salt to the batter and mix.

Grease the inside of two 4-inch by 1¾-inch springform molds with butter. You can peel back the butter wrapper and use it like a giant crayon if that's easiest. Sprinkle the flour into one of the

Continued on page 180

———·· 178 ··———

molds. Tip the mold and rotate it to coat the interior with flour. Pour the remaining flour into the other mold and repeat. Discard any remaining flour.

Place the molds on a parchment paper–lined baking sheet and divide the batter evenly between the molds, tossing in a small handful of chocolate chips after filling each mold halfway.

Preheat an oven to 350°F. Bake for 20 minutes. Test it after 18 minutes. You should see a little wobble in the center of the cakes when you jiggle the baking sheet.

To finish, sprinkle the sliced almonds on top of the chocolate cake. Then put the confectioners' sugar in a small fine-mesh sieve and gently tap it over the cake to give it the pretty white snowy topping.

Almond Paste

YIELD: 200 G (7 OZ)

1½ cup (225 g) almonds
1½ cup (150 g) confectioners' sugar
1 egg white
1 teaspoon (4 g) kosher salt

Add the almonds and sugar to a food processor fitted with the blade attachment and process until smooth, 1 to 2 minutes. It should be the consistency of sand.

Add the egg white and kosher salt to the food processor and process to incorporate, about 30 seconds.

Scoop into an airtight container and refrigerate for up to 3 days or freeze for up to 1 month.

Chocolate Pudding

YIELD: ABOUT 2 SERVINGS

For the Mordecai Glickman dinner, Rose has Zelda whip up a variety of chewing-optional foods. Pudding is among them but, sadly, we don't actually get to see it onscreen.

This light, airy chocolate pudding comes together in no time at all, something I think Zelda would appreciate. If you use a darker chocolate than the 60% called for, feel free to add a few tablespoons of sugar to compensate for the increased bitterness.

4.5 ounces (125 g) 60% dark chocolate
½ cup (110 g) heavy cream
4 (140 g) egg whites

Use a chef's knife to chop the chocolate. Add it to a bowl and set aside.

Bring the cream to a simmer over medium-high heat. Once it simmers, pour over the chocolate and whisk to combine. Set aside to cool.

In a separate bowl, use an electric hand mixer to beat the egg whites to stiff peaks. If you're new to the baking world, turn the mixer over so the paddle attachments point up. Does the egg white on the paddles keep its peaks? If not, continue beating.

Fold the beaten egg whites into the chocolate mixture one-third at a time. To fold: use a spatula to pull one-third of the egg whites into the bowl containing the chocolate, insert the spatula into the center of the bowl, and fold in the egg whites. Turn the bowl 90 degrees and repeat. Once incorporated, repeat with the remaining egg whites. The goal here is to gently mix without deflating the egg whites.

Top with extra Harissa-Candied Almonds (page 73), or a generous pinch of Maldon sea salt.

Crème Fraîche Cheesecake

Why does everything have to be so sweet all the time?

I want bitter. Give me bitter. And sour. Maybe a little salty in there for good measure. I'm done with all the sweet.

Where did we go wrong?

America loves sugar. Ohhh boy, do we love sugar. And can you blame us? It's the sweet white powder. Our Cromag brains go bonkers when we taste sugar.

Enter this dessert. This is a dessert for people who don't like things too sweet. It looks sweet. Sounds sweet. But it's not too sweet. A lot like Midge. She looks like a nice, normal 1950s housewife but when she gets on stage, there's a whole other side of her.

---

4 ounces (114 g) cream cheese
¼ cup (100 g) crème fraîche
1½ tablespoons (40 g) sugar
¼ cup (60 g) heavy cream
½ vanilla bean
1 egg

For the Graham Cracker Topping:
8 (60 g) graham crackers
½ cup (60 g) pistachios
1 stick (113 g) butter
Salt, to taste

Continued on page 186

For the cheesecake

Use an electric hand mixer to beat the cream cheese and crème fraîche in a large bowl until smooth. Add the sugar and cream and beat to mix until smooth again. Use a paring knife to cut a vanilla bean in half and reserve the other half for another use. Slice down the vanilla bean half to open the bean and expose the seeds inside. Take care not to cut all the way through the vanilla bean. Open the pod by folding the sides back and slide the knife down the length of the bean to scrape out all the seeds. Add them to the bowl along with the egg and beat to combine.

Preheat the oven to 325°F. Put the mix in a 4-inch by 1¾-inch springform pan, place it on a parchment paper–lined baking sheet, and put it in the oven. Bake until the cake is set, about 25 to 30 minutes. It should still wobble a bit in the center.

For the topping

Add graham crackers and pistachios to a food processor fitted with the blade attachment. Process until it's a fine meal.

Add butter to a small skillet over medium heat. It'll melt, then bubble, then bubble smaller bubbles. When it smells nutty, remove from heat and pour into the graham cracker mixture.

Stir. It'll look like wet sand. After it cools a moment, taste it and add salt to taste. I usually add ½ teaspoon, but add as much or as little as you like. Refrigerate until ready to serve, at least 2 hours.

Salted Caramel Sauce

YIELD: 1 CUP

1 cup (200 g) sugar
2 tablespoons (30 g) water
½ cup (100 g) heavy cream
¾ teaspoon (3 g) kosher salt
2 tablespoons (28 g) butter
2 tablespoons (20 g) bourbon

Heat the sugar and water in a saucepan over medium heat without stirring. Let it develop into a deep caramel color.

Pour the cream into the caramel. Be careful—it will bubble violently.

Add the salt, the butter, and the bourbon and stir. Let cool to room temperature and then refrigerate until ready to use.

Parisian Cocoa

YIELD: 1 CUP

"Don't move. Don't think. Just drink."—Rose Weissman.

It sounds like the last thing a fraternity pledge hears before blacking out, but Rose Weissman knows exactly what to tell her daughter after a busy moving day. And what better way to celebrate your daughter and grandchildren moving in with you than Parisian Cocoa.

There are only two ingredients in this recipe, so use good ingredients. Valrhona makes exceptional chocolate. Feel free to experiment with different chocolates if you like.

I highly recommend a sprinkle of finishing salt at the end. Fleur de sel, gray salt, Maldon sea salt—any of these are great options. You can use more flavorful salts such as Himalayan sea salt, black lava salt . . . Try a pinch and see what you think.

———

1 cup (240 ml) whole milk
2½ ounces (70 g) good-quality chocolate, such as Valrhona
Finishing salt, as needed

Bring milk to a simmer in a small saucepan over medium heat.

Add the chocolate to the saucepan, remove from heat, and gently whisk. You're not trying to aerate the chocolate; you only need to mix it together.

Serve in a small coffee cup, demitasse cup, or whatever you've got handy. Top with a pinch of a finishing salt of your choice.

Peanut Butter Cookies

YIELD: 15 COOKIES

After running into Joel and Penny at Foo's, the Weissmans scramble for a good meal at home. Their options? Capers and mustard, cottage cheese that is no longer cottage cheese, a container of brown that could be either soup or gravy, and gefilte fish. Wait, no. Someone stole that . . .

Do yourself a favor and make sure you always have some cookies stashed in your cabinet. They'll come in handy if you ever find yourself in a situation where you run into your ex and his or her new beau at a Chinese restaurant and need to flee. Oh, and don't forget to take the champagne when you rush out. Even if it's already open. (That's why God invented funnels, after all.)

My wife doesn't cook much, but when she does, it's amazing. This is one of the recipes she makes, and I'm thankful she shared it with me. (Hey, Fernie, if you're reading this, I won't mind *at all* if you make these when I come home today/every day.)

* * *

1 cup (250 g) peanut butter
1 scant cup (200 g) sugar
1 egg (~55 g)
1 tablespoon vanilla extract

Preheat the oven to 350°F.

Line a baking sheet with a Silpat or parchment paper. Use a wooden spoon or an electric hand mixer to mix the ingredients together in a large bowl.

Divide the dough into 1½ tablespoon (30 g) portions and roll into balls. Arrange them on the prepared baking sheet, leaving 2 inches between them. Use a fork to make a crosshatch pattern on the tops of the balls. Don't completely flatten then into discs.

Bake at 350°F for 6 to 8 minutes. They will seem undercooked when they first come out of the oven, but they'll firm up as they cool.

Bonus points: Sprinkle a few chocolate chips over the cookies when they come out of the oven to make them taste like a chocolate peanut butter cup.

Zagnut

YIELD: ABOUT 30 COOKIES, DEPENDING ON HOW YOU BREAK THEM

These are for Susie. Maybe she's had a bad day. Perhaps Midge just bombed and needs to be talked off the ledge.

These will not be exactly like the Zagnut candy bar. You can order those from specialty stores online. These are, however, fucking fantastic. I think Susie would argue they're better than the real thing.

7½ (120 g) graham crackers
1 scant cup (225 g or 8 ounces) smooth peanut butter
1 tablespoon (7 g) cocoa powder
1 cup (75 g or 2½ ounces) shredded coconut
2 cups (453 g or 16 ounces) granulated sugar
4 tablespoons (60 g) water

Prep ingredients. Place the crackers on a parchment paper–lined baking sheet. Set aside. Mix peanut butter and cocoa in a small bowl and set aside. Add coconut to a large nonstick skillet and heat over medium heat. Toss or stir until toasted, 5 to 7 minutes.

Make candy. Add sugar and water to a medium-sized saucepan and warm over medium-high heat. Bring to a boil and cook until the sugar reaches 300°F to 310°F, about 15 to 20 minutes. Remove from heat and mix in peanut butter and cocoa powder.

Pour over crackers and use a spatula to coat the crackers in an even layer. Sprinkle toasted coconut on top. Cool completely and then break or cut apart.

A Note from the Author:

Steal Like Nobody's Watching

Socrates was first to coin the phrase *dance like nobody's watching*. He was so ahead of his time.

You know you're talented when you write something so beautiful in a language no one spoke. At least fifteen hundred years passed before someone finally understood Socrates, and another thousand years before people could post it on Instagram.

But Plato, Socrates's dutiful understudy, stole the phrase and, being the stealing stealer he was, changed it to *steal like nobody's watching*. (This is all 100% fact, not fake news at all.)

I'd like to encourage you to do exactly that with these recipes.

See, in the comedy world, stealing is bad. It's bad outside the comedy world, too. I think it's even a commandment. Now that I think of it, I suppose stealing is bad pretty much all the time.

Except right now.

I want you to steal these recipes and make them your own. Read this book, laughing gleefully along the way, and then cook something and wait for the compliments to pour in.

That's how comedy and cooking is different. Stealing is bad in one, mandatory in another.

Make Them Your Own

Every comedian improvises a little bit. Far less than the audience thinks. But more than not at all. Some sets it's 100 percent exactly what I've written. Other times, there's something new that pops up. And then I can add it to my repertoire.

Same goes for cooking.

Use the recipes as general outlines, but I encourage you to make them your own. Substitute ingredients that you prefer.

Don't have crème fraîche for the 837 recipes that call for it in this book? Sub sour cream. Don't like chives? Omit them altogether. Got a special thing for dill? Fine. Do whatever you want with it. I'd rather you use these as guidelines than do everything by the letter and then blame me when it doesn't come out perfect.

Kitchen Essentials

Bar Essentials

- **Dry Gin**. I like Gordon's gin because it's a steal. You needn't spend much money on spirits for mixing cocktails. Fancy gins can be nice in a martini but are often wasted in cocktails because their flavor is overshadowed by the other ingredients.
- **Whiskey**. Buy American (Buffalo Trace or High West are great neat and in cocktails; Old Overholt and Rittenhouse are fantastic ryes). Not because you need to be patriotic—I love me some Canadian Club and Crown Royal—but because American whiskies are the best for most cocktails. Canadian, Irish, and Scotch whiskies have different flavors that don't mix as well in cocktails.
- **Brandy**. Courvoisier and Hennessy aren't just for rappers. They make fantastic cognacs. Cheaper/value brands are also fine for mixing cocktails.
- **Sweet and Dry Vermouth**. Noilly Prat is my favorite for both sweet and dry vermouths. Cinzano and Martini & Rossi are more readily available in national grocery chains and are cheaper.
- **Orange Liqueur**. For the purposes of this book, Triple Sec, Orange Curacao, and Orange Liqueur are interchangeable.
- **Aromatic Bitters**. Angostura is a fine bitters and is available in most grocery stores.

Fridge Essentials

- **Eggs**. All recipes in this book use extra-large eggs but large are just fine too. I buy cage free because I have a guilty conscience.
- **Butter**. Salted or unsalted is fine; I don't really notice much of a difference. *Do not* buy margarine. It might have been popular in the 1950s but so was not wearing a seatbelt.
- **Lemons**. 1 to 2 lemons.
- **Limes**. 1 to 2 lemons.
- **Oranges**. 1 to 2 lemons.
- **Italian Parsley**. I keep mine in a mason jar with water in the fridge. It feels fresh and looks sexy.

Freezer Essentials

- **Chicken Stock** (page 90 for homemade!)
- **Vegetable Stock**

Pantry Essentials

- **Kosher salt**. I prefer Diamond Crystal brand for its uniform crystals. Yeah, that sounds super picky, but it's easier to pinch a few fingers' worth than other brands.
- **Sea salt flakes**. For finishing dishes. The extra salty crunch makes a difference.
- **Extra virgin olive oil or canola oil**. Some cooks yell at people for buying the wrong kind of oil.

  "Canola oil has a higher smoking point!"

  "Canola oil has a clearer flavor!"

  "Canola oil isn't made of virgins!"

  For most people, this won't make a difference. And I am most people. I deep-fry in canola, but use olive oil for everything else. *Tip*: Cheap extra virgin olive oil is fine for all the recipes in this book. Get a squeeze bottle to put it in! They're $2 online and will make your life so much easier. Buy olive oil in opaque containers so there's no chance of light spoiling it.
- **Yellow onions**. Keep 1 to 2 on hand.
- **Garlic**. 1 to 2 heads.
- **Shallots**. 1 to 2 bulbs.
- **Capers**. 1 jar.
- **Yukon Gold potatoes**. I always have a pound of these on hand. Just in case I need to make mashed potatoes after a particularly terrible set.
- **Sugar**. Sugar was huge in Mrs. Maisel's time. While we don't eat as much now, it's good to keep on hand in case you need to make cakes to go with your iced tea. You never know when Susie might drop by!
- **All-purpose flour**.
- **Semisweet or dark chocolate chips**. Also for emergencies . . .

Acknowledgments

To my wife, Lauren, for her understanding while our home smelled like onions (for 2 months), her ability to say "this tastes like grunt" without hurting my feelings, and her patience while I repeatedly interrupted her own writing process to ask "can you make this funnier?"

To my agent, Nicole Resciniti, for believing in me. I have no idea why she took me seriously when I said "I can write a cookbook" but I'm thankful she did. She's also a talented fortune teller. In May of 2017 she said "by this time next year you'll have a book deal." And then in May 2018 I did. (Nic, are you available for parties? Do you know what I'm thinking right now?)

To my editor, Nicole Frail, and the entire Skyhorse Publishing team, for turning my steaming pile of words into this beautiful book. And for having the coolest name in publishing. (Am I the only one who thinks Skyhorse sounds like an animated superhero? *Skyhorse to the rescue!*)

To the creators, cast, and crew of *The Marvelous Mrs. Maisel.* Without your hard work and enchanting story this book wouldn't make any sense. Also, thanks for casting me as an extra in season 2. Sorry I drank all my prop cocktail before the shot and kept almost "accidentally" bumping into principal characters.

About the Author

Anthony LeDonne is an author, comedian, actor, and game show host. If he's not in the kitchen or doing stand-up comedy, he's making cocktails for his high school sweetheart and plus-sized Pomeranian in their tiny apartment in New York City.

Index

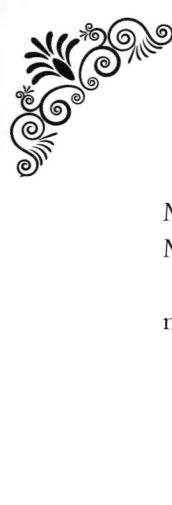

Conversion Charts

METRIC AND IMPERIAL CONVERSIONS
(These conversions are rounded for convenience)

Ingredient	Cups/Table-spoons/Teaspoons	Ounces	Grams/Milliliters
Butter	1 cup/ 16 tablespoons/ 2 sticks	8 ounces	230 grams
Cheese, shredded	1 cup	4 ounces	110 grams
Cornstarch	1 tablespoon	0.3 ounce	8 grams
Cream cheese	1 tablespoon	0.5 ounce	14.5 grams
Flour, all-purpose	1 cup/1 tablespoon	4.5 ounces/0.3 ounce	125 grams/8 grams
Flour, whole wheat	1 cup	4 ounces	120 grams
Fruit, dried	1 cup	4 ounces	120 grams
Fruits or veggies, chopped	1 cup	5 to 7 ounces	145 to 200 grams
Fruits or veggies, pureed	1 cup	8.5 ounces	245 grams
Honey, maple syrup, or corn syrup	1 tablespoon	0.75 ounce	20 grams
Liquids: cream, milk, water, or juice	1 cup	8 fluid ounces	240 milliliters
Oats	1 cup	5.5 ounces	150 grams
Salt	1 teaspoon	0.2 ounces	6 grams
Spices: cinnamon, cloves, ginger, or nutmeg (ground)	1 teaspoon	0.2 ounce	5 milliliters
Sugar, brown, firmly packed	1 cup	7 ounces	200 grams
Sugar, white	1 cup/1 tablespoon	7 ounces/0.5 ounce	200 grams/12.5 grams
Vanilla extract	1 teaspoon	0.2 ounce	4 grams

OVEN TEMPERATURES

Fahrenheit	Celsius	Gas Mark
225°	110°	¼
250°	120°	½
275°	140°	1
300°	150°	2
325°	160°	3
350°	180°	4
375°	190°	5
400°	200°	6
425°	220°	7
450°	230°	8